A Handbook of
PARISH PREACHING

by

GORDON W. IRESON

Warden of the Community of the Holy Name
Formerly Canon Missioner of the Dioceses of
Newcastle and St Albans

MOWBRAY
LONDON & OXFORD

Copyright © Gordon W. Ireson 1982

ISBN 0 264 66857 – X

First published 1982
by A. R. Mowbray & Co. Ltd
Saint Thomas House, Becket Street,
Oxford, OX1 1SJ

Phototypeset by Cotswold Typesetting Ltd, Cheltenham
Printed in Great Britain by Biddles of Guildford

Other titles in Mowbray Parish Handbooks series:

Handbook for Churchwardens and Parochial Church Councillors	Macmorran, Elphinstone, and E. Garth Moore
Handbook of Parish Finance	Michael Perry
Handbook of Parish Music	Lionel Dakers
Handbook of Parish Property	Kenneth Elphinstone
Handbook of Parish Work	Michael Hocking
Handbook of Parish Worship	Michael Perry
Handbook of Pastoral Work	Michael Hocking
Handbook of Sick Visiting	Norman Autton

In preparation
Handbook of Parish Liturgy
Handbook of Pastoral Counselling

TO MY WIFE
Whose constructive criticisms of my sermons
have contributed much to the contents of
this book.

Contents

Foreword

There must be few clergymen in the Church of England who know, understand and care about their fellow clergy in parochial situations more than Gordon Ireson. As Diocesan Missioner in Exeter, then Canon Missioner first in Newcastle and then in St Albans, a ministry spread over more than thirty years, he has been at their side to encourage, stimulate and guide. This down-to-earth experience is what makes this book on preaching stand in a class by itself. Its title is apt – *A Handbook of Parish Preaching*. And the publishers are to be congratulated for including it, not among their volumes on preaching, but in the 'Mowbray Parish Handbooks' series. Properly understood, preaching is part of the pastoral office. This book gets it right.

The word 'handbook' in the title is also apt. It is possible to look up in its pages how to begin a sermon, shape it, clothe it with words and end it. There is even an outline of a sermon and the same sermon written out in full. Considering that this book first appeared in 1959 (it has been virtually rewritten now), it is remarkable how the author emphasises the place of story telling in preaching, an insight now being canvassed. He also takes fully into account the fact that much preaching today takes place at the parish communion.

I am glad to write this Foreword. Gordon Ireson and I were both brought up in Norfolk, attended the same school, worked at the same job before ordination, but did not really meet till he assisted me so ably on my teaching staff at the College of Preachers from 1960. His book is a fitting product of a unique ministry. I commend it warmly.

D. W. Cleverley Ford

Preface

Anyone who has the temerity to write a book about preaching suggests that he imagines himself to have mastered the art. Let me hasten to say that I do not suffer from any such delusion. But the circumstances of my ministry have been such as often to give me the privilege of trying to help other men with their sermon-making, some of them in the first years of their preaching, many others at later stages of their ministry. It is this work, sometimes with small groups, sometimes with individuals, that has made me realize how essential it is for a preacher to understand the few simple principles that lie behind all effective communication.

Many young clerics have to preach too often, and under the pressure of this necessity are exposed to the temptation to hand out their recently acquired theological knowledge with insufficient attention to the manner of its presentation and the principles that govern effective communication of ideas from one person to another. Even for those to whom longer experience has given more facility in sermon production, the maintenance of a weekly output year after year is no easy task, and under the pressure of other parochial duties, a man's preaching may easily lose the priority proper to its pastoral importance.

Yet if ever there was a time when preachers needed to understand the art of 'getting across', that time is now. On the one hand there is a growing sense of need for a faith by which to live in a world which has lost its way. On the other, there is the increasing difficulty of getting through to minds cluttered up with far more stuff, thrust upon them by radio, TV and the press, than they can possibly digest.

The basic principles described in the following pages were first set out in a book entitled *How Shall They Hear*, published by SPCK in 1957 and still in circulation in the early 1970s. But so many changes have taken place since then that both the setting and also the sermons that were provided to illustrate the principles in *How Shall They Hear* were becoming increasingly 'dated'. Moreover I have myself had another twenty-five years of preaching, and also the invaluable experience of acting as lecturer and tutor in many of the College of Preachers' residential courses.

Because I believe that the basic principles of preaching remain unchanged, this book is in effect the first part of *How Shall They Hear* rewritten and brought up to date. I am grateful to SPCK for permission to reproduce some of the original publication.

The text-book (and often didactic!) style of these chapters has however been determined more by their subject matter than by the fact that they have been transcribed from brief notes used for lectures. Since this is in large part a text-book, there seems little point in trying to disguise the fact.

It will be obvious that I am an Anglican priest writing for my fellow clergy, and since the subject of the book is preaching in the parish, I have been largely concerned with the preaching ministry exercised by the parish priest. I am fully aware that this responsibility is now shared by an increasing number of readers and as preaching is an essentially pastoral exercise, I hope that some readers may find what I have written of no less relevance to their ministry than that of the clergy. Further, if some ministers in other traditions are not put off by the Anglican setting of this book (after all they stand in much the same pastoral and preaching relationship to their congregations as do vicars and rectors) and find in it something of value, I shall feel more than rewarded.

Three other things need to be said:

1. I have not, as some writers on preaching have done, devoted one or more chapters to the spiritual life of the preacher. I am writing about preaching, not about prayer. But I write on the assumption that if a man is not praying, neither ought he to be preaching. The spiritual life of the

parish priest is the source of his effectiveness in all the several aspects of his work, not only of his preaching, and there seems no reason why a book about preaching should deviate from its proper subject to deal also with prayer.

2.   Because I hope that this book may be of use to readers as well as to clerics, I have with one or two (I hope pardonable and self-explanatory) exceptions avoided most of the technical terms which figure in clerical discussions and theological textbooks.

3.   I am well aware that not all preachers are of the male sex, but I hope that any woman reader or minister who chances on this book will not take exception to the fact that I have consistently referred to the preacher as 'he'. Imagine the syntactical complications of attempting to do otherwise!

Last, but by no means least, I wish to express my gratitude to Miss Mary Warren, who typed the whole of the MS and never lost patience with my frequent changes of mind. I should also like to thank Canon William Purcell for his advice and help, not least in relieving me of the labour of proof correction during a time of indisposition.

Malvern   Gordon W. Ireson

Chapter 1

Preaching – Past and Present

The tradition that no religious service or occasion is complete without a sermon has behind it a long history. Indeed it is no exaggeration to say that the Christian faith is inseparably bound up with preaching. Central to this faith is the belief that God has acted in human history, in creation, in revelation and in the restoration of man, of which events the Bible is the sole record. These events and their significance for human life and conduct have to be declared afresh to each generation. In the Old Testament history is inseparable from prophecy, and prophecy rests upon and interprets the history. God's work is also God's word. When the Christian Church became separated from Judaism the place of preaching in the Christian assembly was not simply an inheritance from the worship of the Synagogue. Preaching was as essential to the New Israel as the Law and the Prophets had been to the Old. It was the declaration of what God had done in Christ bringing to completion the purpose for which Israel was chosen. It was also the exposition of what relationship to God through Christ must mean in terms of everyday life.

The Church spread and grew in response to this proclamation, and from the earliest days preaching was regarded as an essential element in the Eucharist. The earliest

Christian documents of the post-apostolic age bear witness to this inseparability of Word and Sacrament. Justin Martyr, for example, writing in his first Apology to the Roman Emperor Antoninus Pius in the Year AD 155 describes what Christians do at the Eucharist. He begins his account thus: 'And on the day called Sunday, all who live in cities or in the country gather together to one place, and the memoirs of the Apostles or the writings of the prophets are read, as long as time permits; then, when the reader has ceased, the President *verbally instructs, and exhorts to the imitation of these good things.*'

From earliest times, therefore, the sermon, as distinct from cachetical instruction, was regarded as an integral part of the liturgy, interpreting and expanding some part of the liturgical action or lections. Such an interpretation became even more necessary during the early Middle Ages when the Latin of the liturgy was no longer understood by the congregation and required explanation in the vernacular.

It was not until the friars began preaching in the market-place that it ever occurred to anybody that a sermon had any other setting than the parish church, or any other context than the liturgy. Luther himself kept strictly to this tradion, but the reformers who followed him tended increasingly to separate the sermon from the Eucharist and to make it the centre of non-sacramental Sunday worship. Nevertheless throughout the whole of Christian history until the seventeenth century the sermon was regarded as essentially an exposition of Scripture. The man who broke with this tradition in England was Archbishop Tillotson (1630–1694) whose moralistic discourses introduced what might be called 'the religious essay' or 'discourse on a theme' type of sermon, a fashion which was followed by many eighteenth century preachers and has left a permanent mark on the Anglican type of preaching. Preachers in the present century cannot but be acutely aware that they are addressing a generation for whom the Bible has lost its old authority, and who are accustomed to a daily diet of the disconnected tit-bits of modern journalism. The last few years, however, have witnessed many brave attempts to secure a more integral relationship between the sermon, the Bible, and the liturgy, and this is doubtless to be welcomed.

The fact remains, however, that despite the efforts of many preachers to keep abreast of rapidly changing fashions of thought, the twentieth century has witnessed a serious decline in the importance formerly attached to preaching. To some extent this was an inevitable result of the social, cultural and scientific revolution through which we have passed. At the beginning of the century, especially in the rural communities, the Sunday services and sermons were the only meeting place and 'entertainment' available to the vast majority of people, many of whom were 'Christians' by convention, custom or social sanction rather than by deliberate choice. To say this, however, is not to belittle the profound effect that the Sunday services and sermons had on personal life and conduct. To vast numbers of people they gave meaning to lives that were otherwise drab and toilsome, and the hope of heaven hereafter. To many they kept alive a deep devotion to Christ as their personal saviour. The advent of cars, radio, TV, hobbies, etc., now offer what to most people are much more exciting alternatives. Today those who go to church or chapel do so by deliberate choice and conviction. You would therefore expect that, for them at least, the sermon would have gained in importance as a means of strengthening their faith and resolve to continue swimming against the tide of secular fashion. But, oddly, it has not. It is not that sermons have not been preached. They have. No service is regarded by the congregation as complete without one. Nevertheless the sermon has fallen in the esteem of both preachers and congregations. It is not easy to see why this is so. Pulpit and pew have reacted on each other. Poor sermons have produced low expectations from the congregation which in turn have called forth diminished effort on the part of the preacher.

I have had the opportunity of asking very many clergy how much and what kind of training in preaching they received in their theological college. Their answers indicate that while some colleges provided considerable and useful help, that offered by others was neglible. But no single theological college seems to have provided a training in preaching which, in my view, is in any way commensurate either with its pastoral importance or with the time and effort which the men, when they are ordained, will have to spend in preparing and preaching sermons.

As a member of the bishop's diocesan staff in three dioceses I have been regularly involved in consultations about appointments to vacant benefices. In over thirty years I could count on the fingers of two hands the number of times the question was asked about a particular candidate 'Is he a good preacher?'.

How has this change in our attitude to preaching come about? Some would point to the theological upheaval of the 60s as the period when many preachers became confused about the grounds and content of their faith. But we are not now living in the 60s. The events of the last decade and the evident inability of modern man to solve the problems of his own making have produced a very different mood. Enthusiasm for *The Secular City*[1] has given way to widespread cynicism and despair. The threat of possible nuclear war paralyses our thoughts and plans for the future. Our civilisation seems to be drifting towards a disaster which we are powerless to avert. There is now little pressure on theologians to accommodate the Christian faith to the presuppositions of a secular society whose values and assumptions are now so clearly under judgment. In this respect the theological climate, apart from a minority of vocal radicals, is much less confused and more positive. The greatest change in the place and pattern of our preaching has been the growth of the Parish Communion and the decline of Evensong.

[1] The title of a book by Prof. Harvey Cox, published in 1965 and described by a reviewer as 'A Christian acclamation of both the emergences of secular urban civilization and the breakdown of traditional religion.'

THE PARISH COMMUNION

At the 11 o'clock Mattins or Sung Eucharist the sermon was a full-dress affair preached from the pulpit. Indeed, Sunday Mattins and Evensong were both regarded as preaching occasions, the sermon being the climax of the service.

In the Parish Communion the sermon was seen as subordinate and preparatory to the eucharistic action. Further, since it immediately followed the epistle and gospel the sermon tended to be linked directly to the one or the other, and was often little more than a re-telling of the gospel incident with a simple moral application attached, an exercise making little demand on the preacher. The emphasis on the Parish Communion as 'The Family Service' resulted in the presence of many small children against whose voices and fidgetings the preacher found himself in constant competition. This combination of factors tended to reduce the time allotted to the sermon. A further desire for intimacy and informality increasingly resulted in the use of a central altar and disposed the preacher to preach not from the pulpit but to address the people from the head of the nave, thus making the use of notes more difficult.

Now I do not deny the immense gains that these changes have brought. My only present concern is that they have so often reduced the sermon to the level of a pious and impromptu little homily that could be dispensed with without loss to anyone. Indeed, some clergy deliberately played down the sermon in the supposed interests of catholicity; their argument being that the Eucharist itself is the proclamation of the Gospel. The more recent decline in the practice of Sunday evening worship has further reduced the preacher's opportunity to exercise a ministry of systematic, well-thought out, preaching. This is a highly unsatisfactory state of affairs and we shall have to consider later what can be done to rectify it.

IS THE DAY OF PREACHING OVER?

The changes in the life of the Church are, however, small by comparison with the changes that have been brought about by the social, cultural, economic and scientific revolution through which we are passing. In two generations the circumstances of human life have changed to such an extent as almost to have produced a new kind of man. One has only to compare the life of the average man today with that lived by his grandparents to see how revolutionary this change is, and there is no point in enlarging on it except in so far as it concerns the preacher.

There are those who tell us that the day of preaching is over; that the fifteen or twenty minute monologue 'six feet above criticism' has been rendered obsolete by the modern techniques of publicity and propaganda, television and advertising, which are now so much a part of our daily lives.

It is certainly true that of these revolutionary changes it is the subtle and all pervading influence of the media which most affects our mental and cultural climate. Two of these merit our particular attention.

(a) *The competition for our attention*

If the limited and restricted world in which our forefathers lived provided them with insufficient material to occupy their minds (though this is a pretty large 'if') it is certainly the case that we suffer from a surfeit. Too much is happening and being thrust upon our attention. There are too many claims competing for our interest. We live in a world of IN-MEDIA-CY. There is an earthquake in Italy or a factory explosion in Japan and it is in our news bulletins and on our TV screens within a few hours or even minutes. The agonies of the refugees in Somalia, the current scandal of the cabinet minister who leaked confidential information to the press, the chatter of comedians and the seductive sexiness of the 'commercial' advertising the latest skin lotion are all paraded before our eyes and ears within minutes. There is a limit to the number of things that the mind can assimilate in a given period of time. But the amount of stuff that claims our attention through the media of radio, newspapers, periodicals, and advertisements, is so vastly in excess of this that people's minds tend increasingly to become a kind of television screen having a semblance of life only so long as it reproduces what is received from some external source, and which goes blank as soon as the current is switched off. The greater the number of competitors for our interest, the more necessary does it become to catch the attention with the maximum appeal to sex, sensation, or self-interest, and with the minimum demand upon our processes of thought.

What is the effect of all this pressure, speed and noise upon our minds? It still takes nine months to produce a baby, cows still walk at the same slow pace. Is there not some natural limit to what our minds can cope with? Is there a direct connection between the high incidence of mental, emotional and psychological breakdowns and the nightmare world in which we live?

It may be that practising Christians are less exposed to these dangers than those who are not subject to any personal discipline or have not clearly recognised priorities. The habit of daily prayer should at least result in some sense of perspective. Nevertheless, the Christian layman cannot escape from the mental and emotional climate in which he lives. Neither can the preacher.

(b) *Distrust of public oratory.*

The other aspect of the impact of the modern media in so far as it relates to preaching is the daily misuse and manipulation of the power of speech, which tends to create a widespread, though often unconscious, distrust of public oratory as such. We see the slick politician who never gives a straight answer to a question, but smothers the point at issue with a spate of verbal diarrhoea which sounds impressive but says nothing. We listen to the spokesman of this or that sectional interest using emotive language and fashionable jargon to inculcate attitudes and judgments based on no rational foundation. The preacher likewise must deal in words, and words for many people today are a debased coinage.

A depressing prospect? It might indeed seem that if the day

of preaching is not already over, at least there is no future in it. Small wonder that when under the initiative of Dr Donald Coggan, then Bishop of Bradford, a few of us felt constrained to form ourselves into the nucleus of a College of Preachers with the avowed intention of trying to recover confidence in, and raise the standard of, preaching, there were many who assured us that we were flogging a dead horse.

As it has turned out the pessimists were wrong. During its first ten years more than a 1,000 clergy journeyed to the South of England to put themselves *in statu pupillari* at residential courses, under the leadership of Canon Douglas Cleverley Ford and his assistants, followed by a steady stream of letters of gratitude for the practical help given. The experience of the College of Preachers is but one instance of a widespread revival of interest in preaching, not least in the Church of Rome. The last few years have seen the publication not only of books of sermons but of books about the art and technique of preaching, the preparation and delivery of sermons, many more of which have appeared on the continent than in this country. Contrary to all expectations preaching is beginning to recover its traditional place in the life of the Church.

The first step in this recovery is to clarify our minds about what preaching *is,* what the preacher is *doing* and what the congregation is expected to do in receiving and responding.

Chapter 2

God, The Preacher and The Congregation

Preaching is a mysterious business. On the purely natural level there is little to distinguish it from any other act of public speaking, except its religious content and its ecclesiastical setting. Its ingredients are the preacher, the sermon and the congregation. The fact that the preacher must deal in words, which are ephemeral things, subject to the limitations and hazards of possible misunderstanding, is equally true of any public speaker. Similarly, every speaker, if he is to achieve his purpose, must establish a rapport with his hearers. What distinguishes preaching from all other kinds of public speaking is that to each of these ingredients, the preacher, his words, his congregation and the relationship between speaker and hearers, there is an added dimension – the God in whose name and service the whole exercise takes place, the God whose Spirit is at work in each and all of them. This 'supernatural' dimension (and we have to call it that to distinguish it from the simply natural and human activity) defies definition. It cannot be controlled and is wholly unpredictable. Our only way of trying to appreciate (I cannot say 'understand') God's part in this mysterious activity is to think of it in relation to each of its natural ingredients.

Even this piecemeal approach is much more difficult than

it might appear. It would be easy to write about preaching in idealistic terms, treating only of the preaching that is spiritually effective, and ignoring its all too human limitations and failures. But to do this would be less than honest and, more importantly, would fail to do justice to the fact that God works not only through the preacher and his congregation, but often in spite of them. I fear that this attempt will result in a somewhat diffuse chapter, but I hope that the reader's patience will not be entirely without reward.

WORDS!

Let us begin with the fact, referred to in the previous chapter, that the constant misuse and manipulation of words to further political and sectional interests has led to a widespread distrust of public utterance, and that this distrust is often, if unconsciously, extended to the pulpit. Nevertheless, we cannot dispense with words. They are the chief means of our communication with each other. It has often been remarked that speech and the use of words is one of the abilities which most distinguishes man from the rest of creation. Indeed, the German philosopher Martin Heidegger claimed that it is not so much that man creates language as that language creates man. The ability to put thoughts into words, and so to communicate ourselves to others is the way by which we become persons. 'Language,' he says, 'is the voice of being and is what distinguishes the authentic person from the unauthentic masses who are content with hearsay and the repetition of clichés.' A man's words are the expression not only of his thinking (or lack of it) but also of himself. So speech is the way of growth in personality. Moreover, there are times when everything – literally everything – hangs on a word:
'Darling, will you marry me?'
'Do you find the prisoner guilty or not guilty?'
'Tell me, Doctor, do you think she'll live?'
There is of course a vast difference between the spontaneous, uninhibited use of language in everyday relationships at home,

at work, and among friends and acquaintances and in its more conditioned and considered use in public. Hence the attention given to a speaker in public is conditioned by fewer factors than those which operate in the complexities of personal relationships.

In the case of public utterance there are in general only two relevant considerations. One is the speaker himself, the regard in which we already hold him or our own personal relationship (if any) with him, or (if we have no such knowledge or relationship) the confidence which his words or manner inspire. The other is the relation of what he is saying to our own lives and interests. I may have no relationship with the speaker and no particular reason for trusting or mistrusting him; but if the subject on which he is speaking is of personal concern to me – the rate of income tax in the new budget, the town plan that is going to rob me of part of my garden, or new treatment for a complaint from which I suffer – then I shall give him my undivided attention. Similarly if he is speaking on a subject in which I am already interested, or if he manages immediately to enlist my interest, even if I am disquieted or horrified by what he says, I will listen so long as he holds my interest. Words are live when the issues are live. The Gospel is concerned with issues that are basic to human life and destiny, but it will only be heard if its proclamation makes this relevance unmistakably clear.

Yet how much preaching has been about topics that may be interesting to the preacher, if not to his congregation, but not essential to holding the Christian faith or living the Christian life. It has been said that many clergy spend their time answering questions that their congregations are not asking. They are like radio stations transmitting on a wave-length to which no receivers are tuned. I don't believe this to be true of the majority either of our present day clergy or our readers. But I have myself heard very many sermons of which this criticism was fully justified. For this kind of preaching there is no future. So, how does the preacher ensure that he is dealing with vital issues and not simply handing out platitudes? How does he inspire the trust accorded to a friend rather than the detached caution if not cynicism so often accorded to a public speaker?

PREACHING IS PERSONAL AND POSITIVE

Let me begin with another question. Is the verb 'to preach' transitive or intransitive? The dictionaries allow it to be both, and usually give precedence to its intransitive usage – 'to sermonize, to give advice in an offensive, tedious or obtrusive manner' etc. But in the New Testament 'to preach' is always used as a transitive verb. The object is either stated or implied. It is to preach the Gospel, to preach Christ, to preach repentance and remission of sins, to preach the Word of God. But no preacher can do this unless he speaks from his own experience of these things. He cannot preach the Gospel as something external to himself.

Preaching is essentially personal. It is also essentially positive; a bearing of testimony to things that are. The contemporary preacher is concerned no less than were the first apostles to bear witness of our Lord's Resurrection, not only as an historical fact, but also as an abiding experience. And while they could claim, as we cannot, to have been eyewitnesses of the first resurrection *appearances,* we for our part can point, as they could not, to the witness of many centuries of Christian experience. Such positive testimony clearly carries more weight than any number of negative arguments. Suppose a man is up before the magistrate on a charge of assault and battery, but he denies having committed any such offence. Two witnesses are then called who declare how they saw the prisoner knock the woman down. The magistrate then turns to the man in the dock and says: 'Well, Smith, here are two men who clearly saw you knock her down. What have you to say to that?' There would be little point in his replying: 'Well, your Worship, I can produce twenty-two people who *didn't* see me do any such thing.' The positive testimony of those who say, 'I know that the Christian faith is true because I've proved it so in experience', has considerably more evidential value than the doubts of those who say, 'I don't think there's anything in religion, because I've never found it'. We more readily listen to a man who obviously knows what he is talking about than to the man who admits that he doesn't. The preacher, by the exercise of his function, articulates a great weight of positive testimony, both of the historic Christian community standing invisibly behind him and also of the conviction that he himself brings to his task. 'I stand for what I say, and I stand by it.'

I am not, of course, suggesting that the preacher should talk about his own spiritual experiences.[1] All I am concerned to say is that preaching is essentially a personal approach to persons, a man speaking to his fellow men. No matter what subject he may be dealing with – the authority of the Bible; the message of Amos; the meaning of the Eucharist; the Church's ministry of healing – he will not simply be handing out information in an impersonal manner, like the clerk at the station inquiry office who tells you what train you can get from where. He will speak as one who is personally committed; as one who cares intensely for the Bible; as one to whom Amos is a spiritual ancestor; as one who knows from first-hand experience that our Lord is to be found in the Eucharist, and his power in the healing ministry. It is not so much what he actually says that will convey this conviction as the way in which he says it. And what he manifestly is will count for even more than what he says. Nothing could be farther from my mind than any suggestion that we attract people by our personality. Such exponents of this notion as I have met make me want to pronounce the word as some Americans do –

---

[1] There is, however, a place for the preacher's personal testimony, 'I know from experience that this is true, and so will many of you,' etc. I have never forgotten the profound impression made on me many years ago by a dear old Archdeacon who prefaced a sermon one Sunday morning by saying: 'My friends, it is in my heart to tell you that I have been ordained fifty years today and never once in all that time has our Lord failed me, though I have often, alas, failed Him.'

'poisonality'! But while preaching is not simply or chiefly a matter of personality, it *is* personal, and can never be impersonal. It is a man testifying to his fellow men of what God has done, ' . . . that which we have heard . . . that which we have seen with our eyes, and our hands handled . . . declare we unto you.'[1] Our Lord made no provision for the communication of his Gospel other than this. 'Go ye therefore, and make disciples of all the nations. . . .[2] Ye shall be my witnesses . . . unto the uttermost part of the earth.[3] He that heareth you heareth me.'[4] The preacher is a man sent to tell somebody else of what he knows. Preaching, therefore, is a man speaking not from the heights of a superior culture, but from the depths of personal conviction. He preaches not only because he holds a commission to deliver a message, but because that message holds him.

GOD SPEAKS THROUGH MEN

The preacher is a man speaking about God to his fellow men, and in doing so he must master and make use of the principles of effective communication. But both in the New Testament and in Christian tradition the act of preaching is conceived as a way by which God himself speaks to men. There can be few preachers who have not discovered the profound truth of this apparent paradox. If any sermon of mine brings another man to Christ, the one thing I can be quite sure about is that it is God's doing, not mine. This is the mystery and miracle of preaching. It takes place at two levels, the natural and the supernatural. It is sacramental, the outward and audible instrument of an inward and spiritual grace. As St Paul argues, 'the word of the Cross is folly to the natural man, but to us who are being saved it is the power of God. For since in the wisdom of God, the world did not know God through wisdom, it pleased God through the folly of what we preach to save those who believe.'[5]

[1] 1 John 1. 1, 3
[2] Matt. 28. 19
[3] Acts 1. 8
[4] Luke 10. 16
[5] 1 Cor. 1.21

Spiritual truths are spiritually discerned. How does God speak through a man? How did he speak through the prophets? By inspiration (literally) not only of the speaker but also of the hearer. This did not make the prophets infallible. There are prophecies in the Old Testament which taken literally were never and now can never be fulfilled. But this did not invalidate the essential burden of their message, either for those who have the grace and humility to receive it, or for those of us who read their words many centuries later. We have, and always have had to rely on human testimony, even on what we know about the words of the Incarnate Word himself. But it is the Holy Spirit who preserved the integrity of the witnesses, and interprets it to each succeeding generation. The Word of God comes through men, but it does not exist in a vacuum. It is adressed to men who, as Our Lord pointed out in the parable of the sower, may receive it with varying degrees of acceptance or rejection. The preaching of a sermon is a two-way activity; it is a reciprocal relationship between preacher and congregation, operating as has been said on two levels, the natural and the supernatural or spiritual.

I have said that the ministry of the Word is sacramental. It might be more accurate to say that it is incarnational. The elements or instruments of the Eucharist are impersonal. They are things – bread and wine – which can neither resist nor cooperate with the sacramental purpose for which they are used. But the preacher is a man with a will of his own and a mind of his own. He may or may not be an effective instrument in God's hands. Suppose we regard him as a pompous ass, or distrust his scholarship or have grave suspicions about his orthodoxy? How can we listen to him as we listen to a man of infectious faith and shining holiness? The answer is that we do not. We probably cease attending altogether and think of other things! Suppose however that we find ourselves disturbed by a preacher who seems to be casting doubt upon the reality of the Incarnation or the truth of the Resurrection? What then? Is it that our hold on the faith is so tenuous that we cannot bear to have it undermined any more? Or is it because the Spirit is using this sermon to strengthen our faith and re-examine the foundations on which it rests? It could be either. But before we jump to the conclusion that it is the former, let us consider the number of congregations who remain faithful to their Sunday worship throughout the incumbency of a priest whose preaching is incompetent or mischievous or both. Examination of the history of such a congregation will I believe, in the vast majority of cases, reveal that at some time, in the ministry of some past incumbent, they have caught a vision of the truth as it is in Christ and his Church and are determined to remain faithful.

The converse is equally true. We have all known congregations which for years have been spiritually starved and where worship has become merely habitual, come to new life under an incumbent who can communicate his vision through preaching and pastoral care. In so far as it is possible to generalise from such particular experiences and observations there are I think two truths of the highest importance to the preacher:

1. Preaching is essentially a reciprocal relationship between preacher and congregation in which the part of the latter is as important as that of the former. It is the congregation which governs how much of what the preacher gives is actually received. The preacher's job is to win from the congregation the maximum readiness to receive. Equally, the initial readiness of the congregation can 'pull out' of the preacher, every bit of what he has to give.

2. Every congregation has an individual character or spirituality born of its past history. This past history will almost certainly contain alternations of vicars who have been effective spiritual leaders and teachers, and those who have not. My contention is that it is the positive work of the effective priests which leaves a more lasting mark on the congregation than the lean years of the ineffective ones. I believe that this is one of the ways in which the work of the Holy Spirit is discernible in a congregation. Nor must we overlook the incalculable

effect of the regular sharing in the worship of the Church – the Scriptures, the prayers and, most important of all, the presence of our Lord promised to those who are gathered together in his name. The preacher may be an ass; it was an ass that carried Our Lord to Jerusalem. He is certainly a sinner like the rest of us, but God can use asses as he uses sinners. And however poor and inept the sermon, there are saints in the congregation who will be praying.

I am not suggesting that the holiness and competence of the officiant and the preacher are not important. They obviously are. But, so equally is the attitude and approach of the congregation. Having served as diocesan missioner in three dioceses it has been my privilege to have worshipped with and preached to a large number of congregations, with many of which I had a continuing relationship. Each had its own corporate personality. No two of them had the same 'feel'. They varied enormously in their sense of expectation and their togetherness. Indeed I was able (or thought I was) on my first visit to form a fair assessment of the quality of the incumbent's preaching and spiritual leadership, by the spirit of their worship and the sense of expectation or lack of it with which they composed themselves for the sermon before I had even begun.

It would be foolish to deny the natural and human element in preaching. The congregation will learn much from a good teacher, it may be bored or starved by the poor preacher. Indeed if every member of the congregation brought nothing to bear on the sermon but his rational faculties this would be the sum total of the exercise. Yet unless a man is seeking God and is in some degree of relationship with God and with his fellow Christians, why is he in church at all? And once he and his fellow churchmen have even a slender hold on the spiritual dimension, then the natural is interpenetrated by the supernatural. Therin lies the mystery of preaching.

From this point onwards I shall be concerned with the human and natural elements that go to the making of a sermon, the principles of communication which the preacher must observe and the disciplines which he must exercise. But I recognise that this is not the whole story. When in the next chapter I describe the preacher as 'feeding' his congregation I realise that he is providing only the loaves and fishes for the Lord to use. This does not lessen the preacher's responsibility. On the contrary. We are ministering to people living in a secular society, breathing its atmosphere and subjected to the subtle and all pervading pressures of a secular dominated media. Its manipulators may prostitute words and create profound distrust in thoughtful minds. They are nevertheless extremely skilful and we ignore them at our peril. Luther asked, 'Why should the devil have all the best tunes?' We should ask, 'Why should the secularists have all the best skills?' We cannot compete with radio and television in their own field but we can at least try in our own field to match skill with skill. We can ensure that when we preach we are not bungling amateurs, but men who have come to terms with the discipline of effective communication, and dedicated it to the service of the Lord who has called us and our congregations to reflect his glory.

Chapter 3

The Preacher's Purpose

So let us turn to the purely human and natural demands of the preacher's task. What does the preacher think he is doing when he goes into the pulpit or stands in front of the altar to deliver his sermon? Does he regard it as his great opportunity or his weekly tyranny? And what of the congregation? Do they respond in eager anticipation or with resigned boredom? What *ought* the sermon to do for them?

Most of us would agree that the purpose of the sermon is to help the hearer to make a more complete response to Christ, to be a more truly converted soul, to strengthen his life in Christ. There may be many local and particular variations on this theme – for example, it may be that the preacher's immediate concern is that the Christ-centred life of his congregation should express itself in more generous support of the Church overseas. But the overriding purpose of preaching is the making of better Christians.

How, then, does the sermon achieve this end? By stirring the hearer's emotions so that he is, for the moment at any rate, conscious of a warm love for his Lord? By enabling him to get a clearer grasp of some of the great truths of the Faith? By persuading him, by whatever means, to strengthen his resolution to resist temptation and to live more faithfully?

And if the sermon is to achieve any or all of these ends is it necessary that it should be remembered? Ought that moment of religious emotion to remain a cherished memory? If not, has it made any permanent difference? Ought the hearer to be able to recall what the vicar said about the evidence for the Resurrection? If he cannot, did he learn anything from that Easter sermon? And if he has forgotten, has the sermon been wasted? What do those of us who preach hope will happen to the sermon when it has left our lips and impinged on the ears of the hearer?

Some years ago a long correspondence was started in one of the Church newspapers by a letter which ran something like this:

Dear Sir,
    I have been a regular worshipper for over thirty years, and on the basis of two per Sunday I calculate that during this time I must have heard over three thousand sermons. Looking back over my thirty years of Church life, I can honestly say that I cannot now remember a single one of those sermons. I therefore ask myself whether I should have lost much if those sermons had never been preached? I raise this question in no carping or critical spirit. I know how much labour and effort the clergy spend on the preparation of their sermons. My purpose is simply to suggest that the time so spent might be better employed and with no real loss to the congregation.
                                                            Yours etc.,
                                                            Faithful Layman.

As might be expected, Faithful Layman's letter provoked a vigorous and sustained correspondence that was finally (and wisely) closed by the Editor with a letter which ran roughly as follows:

Dear Sir,
    I have been married for over thirty years. Every night when I reach home my wife has ready for me a nicely prepared meal. Looking back over my thirty years of married life, I can honestly

say that I cannot now remember a single one of those meals. But I am quite sure that if I had not had them I should not be the happy and healthy man I am today.

Yours etc.,
John Brown.

That surely is the answer. It is certainly one that would be endorsed by the vast majority of worshippers. But it is an answer by analogy. How far can an analysis of John Brown's analogy serve as a legitimate method of inquiry? Probably no single illustration will cover the whole of what is a highly complicated process, and (let the reader be warned) we shall have to make use of others. But it is worth noting that the analogy of feeding has behind it the authority of both the New Testament and the Prayer Book. 'Feed my sheep', said our Lord to the leader of the apostolic band.[1] 'Take heed unto yourselves,' said St Paul to the elders of Ephesus, 'and to all the flock, in the which the Holy Ghost hath made you bishops, to feed the church of God, which he purchased with his own blood'.[2] A good minister of Jesus Christ must himself be 'nourished in the words of the faith, and of the good doctrine'.[3] So the priest at his ordination is exhorted to 'teach and admonish, to feed and to provide for the Lord's family'. Note that the words 'pastor' and 'pastoral' refer primarily to food, pasture. Hence when a man says, 'I am not a preacher, I'm a pastor' he is talking nonsense. He may not be an outstandingly good preacher, though no one need be a bad preacher if he has the humility and discipline to learn his job. But he is not shepherding his sheep unless he is feeding them. On the physical plane we need food to sustain life. Our spiritual life, our life in Christ needs to be sustained by Word and Sacrament. If, then, we allow that the correspondence between the processes of physical and spiritual nourishment is sufficiently close as to justify our use of the one to help us understand the other, John Brown has made an important point,

[1] John 21. 17 [2] Acts 20. 28 [3] Tim. 4. 6

viz. that the 'meat' of the sermon must be accepted and digested, thus supplying life and energy to the organism. The important thing is not that the act of doing it should be remembered, but that it shall have been done. *What matters about a sermon is not that it shall be remembered but that it shall be received.*

What does *receive,* in this sense, mean? At first sight, it might seem that to receive a truth is a purely intellectual process, and many clergy tend to assume that it is. Indeed, the more acutely a preacher is aware of the need for clear and definite teaching of Christian doctrine, the more he will tend to appeal to the rational judgement of his hearers. Certainly the attempt to secure the consent of the intellect must always be an important element in preaching. A man is unlikely to receive much help from a sermon of which he finds himself thinking, 'That is nonsense!' No man ever became a Christian on purely intellectual grounds, and the preacher must always remember that he is addressing himself not only to people's minds but also to their souls. To say this is not to call in question the rational coherence of the Christian faith. On the contrary, most thoughtful Christians would agree that in the last resort there is only one reason for accepting the Christian faith, and that is because it is *true*. But, in fact, very few of us are equipped for dealing with questions of ultimate truth. If our salvation were dependent upon our ability to find our way through the labyrinth of philosophy and metaphysics, few of us would stand an earthly (though in the providence of God we might stand a heavenly!) chance. We can't wait to 'prove all things.' Life is too urgent, and the process of proving too slow.

Even if we had the native ability to discern the ultimate realities, there would still remain the further difficulty that knowing the truth is not the same thing as doing it. A man has not become a Christian when he has arrived at an intellectual acceptance of the Christian claims. He has yet to come to terms with the Christ. This further and essential step cannot be taken by reason alone. Other functions of his nature must be called into action; other knowledge must be gained by other means. It is as when a man who already understands the theory of the internal-combustion engine has to learn how to drive a car. What is it that separates knowledge from experience? What will carry a man across the gulf that yawns between perceiving the truth and practising it?

Psychology has demonstrated (as Christians have known for centuries) that the mainsprings of human conduct do not lie in the reason, but in the affections, in desire and in the imagination. We are not nearly such rational creatures as we like to suppose. We all tend to act first and provide a perfectly reasonable explanation afterwards. Not only so, but even in the sphere of supposedly intellectual thought our conclusions are often influenced by factors of which we ourselves are unconscious. We tend to see the force of those arguments that support our chosen way of life, and to remain uninfluenced by those that would dispose us to an opposite conclusion. That reason is defective is only too patently obvious. If it were not so, given the same premises, men would reach the same conclusions. But they don't! If anyone doubts that men's actions and arguments are not motivated solely by reason, let him listen to the debates in the House of Commons. Heredity, temperament, education, experience, personal ambition, self-interest, class-prejudice – these, and many other, factors influence our thinking no matter how intellectually disinterested we claim to be.

To the man who stands outside the Christian way of life the case against the truth of the Christian claims will seem as strong as arguments that may be adduced in its favour, and the devil sees to it that any argument that might draw a man towards the Church will be countered by another calculated to keep him away. There may be church services on the radio, but there are also lectures denying the existence of God. There may be occasional sympathetic references to the Church in the local newspaper, but there is also the letter from 'Indignant Reader' saying, 'I was thrown out of such-

and-such church choir when I was thirteen. Was that Christian?' So long as we minister to the fiction that men will only act when they are rationally convinced, we are playing into the devil's hands and flying in the face of the most elementary facts of human experience. Behind the most closely reasoned philosophy, Christian or non-Christian, there lies an initial act of choice which must be made before thinking can begin. It is possible to be an intellectual Christian. It is equally possible to be an intellectual non-Christian. But the difference between the two is not basically intellectual. It can only be described as moral. 'Truth is apprehended by reason: but all Christians would add – as St John does – not by reason alone. Truth for the Christian is more a moral than an intellectual possession. It involves the response of the whole man. Truth is to be learned by discipleship, to be translated into action, to be lived: our Lord, who is the Truth, is also the Way and the Life.'[1]

The preacher's task therefore is not simply to appeal to reason and intellect, but to stimulate desire: to help men not only to see the truth but to want it for their own possession. To say this (let me repeat) is in no way to minimize the importance of reasoned presentation. Nor is it to imply that the preacher who is addressing a congregation of simple, untutored folk should be any less careful about matters of truth and of intellectual honesty in argument than the preacher who is confronted by a congregation of university dons, though reason occupies a much larger place in the lives of the one sort of people than in those of the other. All I am concerned to stress is that the verdict for which the preacher is striving is not *quod erat demonstrandum,* but *hoc est diligendum; hoc est sequendum.* Not *This is what we set out to prove,* but *Here is something to be loved; this is to be followed.*

How is this to be done? If, in Dr C. S. Lewis's phrase, you can never reach a conclusion in the imperative mood from

---

[1] Archbp. Fisher in a sermon at the World Anglican Congress in 1954.

premises in the indicative mood, how does one bridge the gap? For example, reason may tell me that I ought to have a hobby or take some exercise, but it won't make me want to tinker with model engines or chase an elusive ball over a hazardous assortment of greens and bunkers. What may inspire me to want to do these things? Part, at least, of the answer is to be found in the number of men who were first inspired to make model engines by visiting an exhibition of model railways, or whose first interest in golf can be traced to the enthusiasm of a friend. It is when our imagination is fired that we begin to take action. If we are later called upon to justify that action, either to ourselves or to another, we can always find excellent reasons for doing what we want to do. Desire, imagination, enthusiasm – here are the driving forces in human life, and it is these the preacher must seek to arouse.

We have already stressed the fact that, because preaching is essentially a personal approach to persons, the manner of man that the preacher is will count for even more than what he says. The contagion of a strong conviction has always been recognized as a major weapon in the preacher's armoury. Religious knowledge can be taught, but religion is something that must be caught. And this process of catching is partly a matter of personal infection, unconscious and therefore not susceptible to studied cultivation. There is nothing a preacher can do about it except to be a man of prayer and Christian fidelity. It must be every preacher's aim so to let his own faith and experience inflame his presentation of our Lord Jesus Christ as to kindle a similar response in the hearts of his hearers. That this can, and does, happen is the treasured and thankful experience of most preachers. But the essential element in this process is self-forgetfulness. Any attempt to cultivate a pulpit personality, or consciously to exercise any power of personal attraction, would be in the highest degree disastrous.

While, however, it would be fatal for a preacher to try to make himself attractive, it is of the essence of his function to make his message attractive. To imagine that he has nothing more to do than simply to hand out the truth is to expect what Dr C. S. Lewis rightly says is impossible – *viz.* to win a conclusion in the imperative mood from premises in the indicative. But, although 'This is' will never of itself lead to 'I ought' or to 'I want', we may be favourably or unfavourably disposed towards it by the manner of its presentation. The same 'This is' may evoke a 'Yes, rather' or 'Not on your life'. Everything depends on how it is presented. This bridging of the gap between fact and response is the function of a mental process for which psychologists have coined the term *suggestion.* Defined in the psychological maner as 'the process by which ideas are introduced into the mind without having been submitted to the critical faculties', it sounds rather like an underhand way of influencing people against their better judgement. In fact, however, it is only another way of saying that, since desire and imagination are more powerful motive forces than reason, it is to these that you must appeal if you want men to act. It is simply a common-sense device for eliciting a certain desired response without having to resort to argument, and one that people have used in their relations with each other from time immemorial. What mother doesn't use it a dozen times a day in dealing with small children? Little Tommy falls down and grazes his knee. It doesn't really hurt, and if Mummy passes off the incident with a joke and a smile, Tommy will smile too. But if she rushes to pick him up with evident anxiety, he will howl with heart-rending abandon. The vast business of modern advertising depends very largely on the power of suggestion. Like any other method of influencing people, suggestion may be used fairly or unscrupulously: to people's benefit or to their detriment. Yet, whether consciously and deliberately exercised or not, we are all susceptible to its influence. If, not having much knowledge of painting, I visit an art exhibition and find that most of the people in the hall are gathered round one particular picture, the chances are exceedingly high not only that I shall go and join the crowd, but also that I shall come away quite convinced that the picture was far and away the best thing in the whole exhibition. Indeed, I shall probably proceed to find reasons to justify an idea that I have received not by any rational process of comparing that picture with others, but purely by suggestion.

There is no need to multiply examples of a process with which we are all familiar. What I am concerned to say about it is that it is a process which the preacher must learn to use with all the skill at his command. He will, of course, use it with scrupulous fairness. Because he respects integrity he will not, by the use of suggestion, try to elicit a response contrary to the dictates of reason and truth. But he must realize that reason and truth alone will not make men *act*. The preacher's function is to present nothing but the truth as God has revealed it, but to present it in such a way as to win the response of faith, that is, of desire and action. His business is not only with the truth, but with getting it accepted. That is why the main concern of these chapters will be with such matters as the psychology of communication, the technique of presenting ideas, the use of stories, illustrations and the like.

Let us return to the analogy of food. The task of the preacher, like that of the cook, is to make the food attractive. The very best of foods can be off-putting if they are dished up in a crude and unappetizing manner. Nor does the intellectual awareness that the food itself is good make it any more desirable to eat. Anyone who has had to cope with children at meal times will know the deadlock that is reached when the argument, 'This is good for you' is countered with, 'But I don't like it'.

Conversely, the preacher must resist the temptation to provide what is merely pleasing. It is easy to tickle people's fancies and to whet their appetite with chocolate éclairs and rich cakes. But these delights are not the basis of a staple diet. Most men soon discover that they can get the ear of their congregations by sermons on subjects of topical interest. The strong meat of the Gospel, however, is a body of revealed truth, not a few recipes hastily produced to meet a passing crisis or to answer one of the constantly changing 'contemporary questions'. Not that topical and contemporary questions are to be regarded as taboo. Far from it. Our job is to make contact with people's minds, and there are few quicker and more effective ways than by taking as a point of contact some matter of common concern already well to the fore in their field of consciousness. But it is one thing simply to 'deal with' questions of contemporary interest; it is quite another to use such passing interests as avenues of approach to eternal truths, presented in a systematic fashion. This is precisely the point at which the preacher needs to know his job. Like the cook, he must not only provide good food, he must know how to make it digestible.

Let us go a step further. If what matters about a sermon is not that it shall be remembered but that it shall be received – that it is, *digested* – in what does the process of digestion consist? If a sermon has been received, but is no longer remembered, what has happened to it? Psychologists tell us (and everyday experience confirms it) that the mind does not receive ideas as a sack receives potatoes. There is an automatic sorting-out process which arranges our ideas and experiences in groups or constellations. Think of any word, for example, 'rabbit', and at once there is started a train of associations that your experience has led you to connect with it. You may find yourself going off on a line of thought beginning with the reflection that you – or a close friend of yours is – a 'rabbit' at tennis. Or your thoughts may wander off in pleasant memories of the countryside, to be rudely jerked back into a contemplation of man's relation to the natural order by remembering myxomatosis. Or, again, your thoughts may follow an entirely domestic train because your most recent association with rabbits is derived from reading Beatrix Potter stories to your children. These associations are different for each of us by reason of our differing personal experiences and varied interests. Those which come first to the mind are those which are strongest because they belong to a group of ideas that centres upon some emotion or dominant interest. There are very many such groups or constellations in all our minds, and they are interconnected, so that a particular idea may be linked with several groups. For example, you may have all the associations with the word 'rabbit' suggested and many others, but certain groups are closely bound up with your emotional and instinctive life, while others are much more loosely so connected, lying on the outer fringe, as it were, and therefore rarely remembered. Such an organized system of emotional tendencies centred upon some object is called a 'sentiment', and it is the nature of these sentiments that determine a man's character.

The relevance of this piece of elementary psychology to the task of the preacher is twofold.

In the first place, the readiness with which an idea will be accepted by the mind is determined by the extent to which it is seen to belong to, or to harmonize with, a system that already occupies an important place in the hearer's life. The point at issue here is that not only must the idea presented belong to such a group, *it must be seen to belong*. Only so will it seem to be interesting and important to the hearer. Hence the importance of right methods of presentation and approach.

Secondly, to say that our concern as preachers is with the growth of the Christian character means that our task is the formation of a single master-sentiment centred in or directed towards the God and Father of our Lord Jesus Christ. Every word or idea or experience which can be linked to that sentiment, even though the circumstances in which the link was made may be forgotten, tends to co-ordinate the mind, and to give it unity and strength of purpose. Every calling forth of the emotion associated with that sentiment helps to strengthen it and to give it an increasingly important place in a man's life. Perhaps an illustration will help to make this clear. The difference between a bar of steel that is magnetized and one that is not, is that in the former case the molecules have all been made to lie in one direction, in the latter they are higgledy-piggledy. By repeated stroking with a magnet in one direction the molecules can be pulled out of their disorganized condition into a uniform structure, so that the bar itself becomes a magnet. Here is a picture of the preacher's task. Man is a disorganized muddle of desires and ambitions, hopes and fears, pulled in different directions by God on the one hand and by the world, the flesh, and the devil on the other. Our task as preachers is to bring the magnet of God's love and purpose close to man's life, to stroke it again and again in the right direction, gradually pulling the molecules into line, thus bringing order and consistency into his life, and making it responsive and responsible to God. Ideally, every sermon should achieve some part of this lifelong process. If any sermon fails to do so it will be because the magnet has not been brought sufficiently close to effect any pull.

Viewed in this way, the distinction between *kerygma* and *didache,* and between doctrinal and devotional sermons, loses some of its point. There must be an element of both in all effective preaching. The mind must be fed with the strong meat of the Word. Every piece of Christian truth – of doctrine, of Bible, of the unfolding of the divine mysteries – if properly presented will be built into the content of the mind, co-ordinating other knowledge and experience, and so making for unity of knowledge and unity of purpose. But for the truth to be accepted in this way it must be clearly seen to belong to one of those groups or sentiments that are at the centre of a man's life, though it is not necessary that this recognition should be of a logical or rational kind. The hearer may not recognise the logical connection between, for example, his own love for his children and God's love for his creatures. But he can respond immediately to the moral and emotional correspondence, and at once his life is strengthened to some degree in his total response to God. It matters little whether the sermon which accomplished this fraction of his conversion is remembered or not. What does matter is that the sermon should 'connect' with some part of his own mental and emotional life, co-ordinating his thought and giving direction to his feeling.[1] Of course, the more his life is dominated by a master-sentiment centred in Christ and his Church, the more actively will he bring his mind to bear upon every piece of biblical or doctrinal teaching that will fan the flames of his master passion. What the preacher must realize is that, for the vast majority of his congregation, it is of little use his piling on more and more fuel unless he also fans the flame. Conversely, it is of equally small avail constantly to be fanning the flame if he provides no fuel.

The meal, the magnet, the feeding of the fire – there is little point in adding further to these analogies. They all lead to the same conclusion: the meal must be made digestible; the magnet must be brought sufficiently near; the fire needs constant attention, not only to the fuel but also to the flame. This is the preacher's job, and only if its purpose be clearly understood is it profitable to consider how best it may be done.

---

[1] It is important to distinguish such natural contact with the hearer's emotional life (as any reference to courtship, love, marriage, parenthood, art, or music is almost certain to establish) from *emotionalism,* that is, the deliberate attempt by the preacher to arouse strong feeling. There are occasions when this is legitimate, even necessary, so long as the preacher knows where to direct the emotion he has aroused. But a too-frequent use of emotionalism is enervating, and ultimately becomes self-defeating.

Chapter 4

The Principles of Preaching: The Shape of the Sermon

It should be clear from what has already been said that the sermon is a highly specialised form of public utterance. What distinguishes it from any other kind of discourse is not that it is delivered from a pulpit. The special character of the sermon derives from its setting within an act of worship of which it forms an integral part, and from what it is designed to *do*. This we have already considered in the previous chapter. The purpose of the sermon is to declare the Gospel of God's saving action in Christ (*kerygma*), to show what this involves in terms of daily living (*didache*) and to win the assent of the hearer. The sermon must therefore appeal not simply to the mind but to the imagination and the affections, which are the wellsprings of human action.

We all learn from experience that whenever there is a job to be done or a purpose to be achieved there is always a 'right' and a 'wrong' way of doing it. By the 'right' way we mean the simplest and most effective method as distinct from the clumsy and inefficient. Every cook, carpenter, farmer and gardener, every practitioner in every art or craft holds strong views on the practices and processes belonging to his or her particular trade. For many of the operations performed in daily life and in every craft we use tools, knives and forks, saws and chisels, lawn mowers and lathes. Each of these implements is designed for its particular purpose. Imagine yourself trying to eat your soup, from a flat spoon or playing a violin that has no waist! Anyone at all familiar with the field of mechanical engineering will know how often the engineer has to make a special tool to achieve the result he wants. The shape, hardness and temper of the tool are determined by the material on which and the purpose for which it is to be used.

The same considerations apply to preaching. The sermon is a tool or instrument made for the particular purposes we have been considering. There are some who would prefer to classify preaching as an art rather than as a craft. In fact it comes into both categories. The preacher is a craftsman operating in that range of human experience to which the arts also make their appeal. The more of the artist in him, the more effective he will be, so long as his art is disciplined by his craft, and he has learned to use his tools. His basic tool is the sermon itself which must be shaped and tempered to its purpose.

THE SHAPE OF THE SERMON

What do I mean by the SHAPE of the sermon? It is clear that if he is to achieve his purpose the preacher must do – and do effectively – three things:

First and foremost he must REGISTER, that is, he must establish contact with the minds of his hearers. If he fails to do this he will be a voice crying in the wilderness.

Second, he must present his truth in such a way that his hearers can grasp it. It is no use for him to use all the right and proper language if his speech does not convey the right meaning. His task is to make them *see* what he means. In other words he must REVEAL.

Third, he must make clear how the truth with which he is dealing applies to them: what response to it means in terms of their lives. That is to say he must RELATE his doctrine to devotion and duty.

It is these three R's – REGISTER, REVEAL, RELATE – the need to do these three things that determine the shape of the sermon. These three tasks are so fundamental as to justify our describing them as *principles.* Few preachers will be effective until they have so mastered them that their use becomes unconscious. The process of acquiring skill in preaching is not unlike that of learning to drive a car. The learner knows that he has to operate the throttle, the clutch, and the gear lever. At first he has to think consciously about each movement. He must remember, for example, not to move the gear control until he has depressed the clutch. But after a little practice he finds himself going through all the proper actions without conscious thought, and then he can give his mind entirely to the business of arriving at his destination. So it is with preaching. The beginner must learn and consciously apply these three principles, but he soon finds himself utilizing them without conscious awareness that he is doing so. Indeed, it is only when he has mastered them that he can afford to vary their application when opportunity offers, as a driver may depart from the normal method of starting his engine when he finds himself with an exhausted battery standing on a downward gradient.

THE NEED OF A CLEARLY DEFINED PURPOSE

Before going on to discuss these basic principles there is an important preliminary consideration suggested by our analogy. At whatever stage the driver may be in the process of mastering his vehicle, he must know where he wants to go. The same is true of the preacher. The story is told of the student of a certain theological college, where it was the custom for each to write a terminal sermon to be submitted to the principal for criticism. The student had taken his sermon to the principal's study, and sat in the principal's best armchair while the great man read the sermon. After a while it became obvious that the perusal was finished, but the principal said nothing, until the silence became so unbearable that the student burst out, 'Well, sir. It will do, won't it?' 'Do what?' came the reply. Exactly. If the preacher does not know what he is out to do, it is not likely that any of his hearers will.

It is not enough to have a subject. You must also have a reason or purpose for preaching about it. You say to yourself, 'I'd like to preach about Peter's denial'. Or 'I think I'll preach about Thomas's doubt'. The operative question is 'Why?' It is not enough to say, 'It would make a good sermon'. A sermon to do *what?* How does Peter's denial or Thomas's doubt relate to your congregation? Possibly you know the answer before you ask the question. Last week you visited a man in hospital, a regular member of your congregation. He was dying and knew it. But he was troubled in conscience because he believed he had committed an unforgivable sin. Bit by bit the story came out. 'How could I, a professed Christian, have done that? It made nonsense of my whole life. I'll never forgive myself and I find it hard to believe the God can forgive me either'. Mercifully you are able to help him to see that God lets no penitent sinner go unforgiven. He isn't that kind of God. Finally you give the poor chap absolution and leave him with new hope. On the way back from the hospital you say to yourself, 'I wonder how many others there are in poor John's condition, convinced that forgiveness is available to others but not for them – they have put themselves beyond its reach. I really must tackle this problem'. That's why you want to preach about Peter's denial and restoration to discipleship.

Or again, at a recent Thursday evening study group it transpired that Tom Harris really felt himself to be something of a hypocrite and an outsider because he could not accept that Jesus was God in human life. There was no doubt of his respect for Jesus as the best man who ever lived and a model for us all to follow. Tom would like nothing better than to be assured of the Christian claim, but could not bring himself to accept it. Another personal and pastoral need. You try to meet it by preaching about Thomas. Not all sermons are prompted by particular pastoral encounters, but all sermons should have a specific pastoral purpose. Many sermon subjects arise from your own reading and praying and thinking. Your mind has been illuminated by some new aspect of the Incarnation that you have never realised before, and you say to yourself, 'That's tremendous, I'd like to preach about it'. But why do you want to preach about it instead of simply meditating upon it yourself? Presumably because you think it has an important bearing on the Christian life that you want your people to realise. It is by this kind of cross-examination that you begin to clarify your aim, and it is wise to proceed on the assumption that an aim that cannot be expressed in one reasonably short sentence will be insufficiently clear to the congregation. If the aim as first envisaged proves on examination to be too comprehensive, then make two or three sermons of it. Don't attempt to do more than one thing per sermon.

It follows, of course, that not only must the preacher have a crystal-clear idea of what he is trying to do in each particular sermon, he must also have an equally clear conception of what he is trying to do with his preaching as a whole. In other words, he must have a sound working knowledge of the articles of the Creed as a complete corpus of doctrine and of what these truths mean in terms of everyday Christian living. The preacher must, in fact, be a man with a message. If he is, that message will find expression not only in his preaching as a whole, but in almost every sermon that he preaches.

Later we shall have to think about certain practical steps that must be taken if we are to ensure that our preaching as a whole is covering or trying to cover the Gospel as a whole. For the moment we are concerned with the single sermon. So, assuming that we know our Gospel, how are we to get it over? Let us consider our three principles in *the order in which they appear in the finished sermon.* It is important to stress this because, as we shall see later, this is not the order in which they are worked out in the preacher's mind in the process of constructing the sermon.

Assuming then that we know our Gospel, how are we to get it over? Let us consider our three principles.

1 MAKING CONTACT WITH THE HEARER

The inexperienced preacher often finds himself saying, 'I've got my subject, but how do I begin?' He may resolve his own mental strife by beginning with a description of the circumstances in which St Paul wrote the Epistle from which the text has been taken. This may be a logical method of exegesis and proper to the lecture room. But what is logically fitting is not always psychologically right. The preacher's point of beginning is with the people to whom he is speaking. Remember the old story of the Englishman who lost his way on a walking tour in Ireland. Espying an old fellow digging his garden, he called over the hedge and said, 'I say, Pat, how do I get to Ballymena?' Pat looked a bit puzzled and scratched his head. 'Well,' he said, 'If it's Ballymena you are wanting to get to, you shouldn't start from here'. Many years ago, as an occupant of the pew, I often used to feel considerable sympathy for that Englishman. The man in the pulpit was so obviously wanting me to start from a place where I wasn't. Because he was assuming an intellectual knowledge or spiritual development that I had not achieved, the preacher did not take me with him on his journey. Because he was selecting a route doubtless more direct but nearer to the goal than the point from which I was starting, his directions for my journey were of little use. The first principle of effective communication is expressed in what is said of the Good Samaritan: 'He came where he was.' The preacher must start where his hearers are.

But how can he be sure of this? May not each one of his hearers be starting from a different place? In terms of being at different points along the road of Christian maturity, yes. But there are many experiences and ideas that the vast majority, if not all of them, will have in common. It is with one of these common experiences or interests that we must begin, and it is essential that we should understand the psychological process involved.

Suppose that you have been invited to a reception which you fear is going to be rather formal and sticky. You arrive, are announced, and having been presented to your host you look around the groups of people in the room *in search of a familiar face.* If there is nobody present that you recognize you observe the polite conventions and you make your get-away as quickly as is consistent with good manners. But suppose that as your eye roves over groups of guests you see somebody you know. 'There's old Smith. How nice to find him here.' You quickly gravitate towards Smith with the assurance of a welcome that your friendship guarantees. Now, in place of that drawing-room full of people, imagine a mind full of ideas and experiences. As yet outside that mind is the truth or idea (let us call it Mr X) that you as a preacher wish to introduce to the mind. If when Mr X enters the mind *via* the ear, and looking round does not see a single familiar face, he will say to himself, 'This is no place for me', and he will quickly make his escape, in at one ear and out at the other.[1] The preacher's first responsibility is to be a good host, and to take thought for his guests. Before he ushers in Mr X he will make some preparation for his welcome, so that when X appears he will immediately be handed on to the care of Mr Smith: 'I expect you already know Mr Smith. He is a near neighbour of yours, and, like yourself, he is interested in music and mountaineering.' It is not by chance that the first

---

[1] The psychologically enlightened reader may question this statement on the ground that no experience is ever wholly lost; once received into the mind it remains. This claim may be true, but it serves no immediate practical purpose, since, if ideas that appear uninteresting are retained, they are relegated to such a remote corner (on the outer fringe of the group of associated ideas) that they might as well not be there.

part of a sermon is called the *introduction*. This is precisely what it ought to be. It is the introducing of the newcomer into a company *one member of which has already been prepared to receive him.*

It is important to realize that the introduction thus understood is not simply an exordium. It has, of course, long been recognized that a speaker who desires a sympathetic hearing must try to arrest attention and evoke the goodwill of his audience from the outset. The classical orators called this first exercise or overture the *exordium*. 'The first purpose of the exordium is to win the goodwill of the audience, to make them kindly disposed, attentive and ready to learn.'[1] This is true so far as it goes, but it does not go far enough. Obviously the preacher must gain the interest of his hearers before he can do anything with them, and if he does not secure it by his opening words he will find it very difficult to secure it later. But his purpose is not simply to gain interest *qua* interest, but an interest that can be led into the particular channel along which he wishes to guide it, without abatement. It is easy enough to open up some topic of general interest. But unless it has some integral connection with the subject to be dealt with, there is a grave risk that the interest may be lost in the process of transition, and the sermon will seem disjointed.

This does not mean that the preacher will develop a stereotyped method of beginning his sermon, or that the passage from the introduction to the subject will always follow the same pattern. The more he varies his introductions, the better.

For example we often set out to 'answer' some commonly expressed but essentially theological question, e.g. the problem of suffering or the relation between human freedom and divine providence. We need to get directly to the question as quickly as possible. But suppose we start off, 'One of the greatest obstacles to Christian faith today in the minds of many people is the fact and extent of human suffering. They

[1] Paul Bull, *Preaching and Sermon Construction,* p. 151.

ask "Why does God allow it? why doesn't he do something
to stop it?"' This is too bald. There will be few members of
the congregation to whom the question is not a very real one.
Nevertheless to plunge in at the deep end in *conceptual terms*
may not immediately engage the minds of some already pre-
occupied with other more personal concerns. The question
needs to be raised in a manner more related to every day
experience.

'Well – don't just sit there – DO something'. That, I hasten to
add, is a quotation not an injunction. But how often have we
heard those words, uttered in annoyance or exasperation? You
may even have said them yourself, when you are in some obvious
difficulty or distress, while somebody else looks on and does not
lift a finger to help. It's a natural reaction in the presence of
someone who could come to the rescue but doesn't. And the
most common target of such exasperation and desperation is
God himself. All down the ages men have made such protests
against God. 'O God, why don't you DO something? The times
are out of joint. The forces of evil are getting the upper hand.
Men are flouting you to your face. You soon won't have any
believers left. Why don't you DO something?' You'll find plenty
of such protests in the Bible, not least in the Psalms . . . etc. etc.

Suppose, however, that the subject of the sermon is not
straightforward, 'Why does God allow suffering? – He has
no alternative if we are to be free and to have a mind and will
of our own', but the slightly more subtle subject of the
predicament of man and the providence of God. The
preacher might engage the minds of his congregation in some
such manner as this:

Have you ever come to any conclusion about Joan of Arc? Do
you think that her voices were genuine? That she really was
moved by God to do what she did? Who was right – the people
who condemned her as a witch and a heretic or those who
twenty-five years later declared her innocent, or those who
ultimately canonized her as a saint?
    I select Joan of Arc as an illustration of the theological
problem I have in mind, because the enemy from which she

delivered France was England. In time of war, if there is some manifest justice in our cause, we all tend to think that God is on *our* side. In the hundred years war he seems to have been on the side of France. Or was he? In human strife, in bloodshed and battle is God ever on anybody's side?

On the face of it, there is a great deal in the Bible to suggest that he is, or can be. The history of the people of Israel is one long story of fighting for existence. They had to fight for their right to settle in the promised land of Palestine, and then to defend themselves against the great rival empires of Egypt, Assyria and Babylon. Indeed they only survived against incredible odds because of their conviction that God was on their side. It was God who had rescued them from slavery in Egypt; it was God who raised up Joshua, Deborah, Barak, Gideon, Jepthah, Saul and David to defend them against the Edomites, Amalakites, Philistines and others. So they believed. Were they right or wrong? Had they entirely misunderstood his will, or did God, so to speak, change his tactics, so that in many pages of the Old Testament he appears to be a very different God from the father of our Lord Jesus Christ? It is a question from which we cannot escape every time we read one of the more blood-thirsty passages of the Old Testament. It's a question to which the *wrong* answer has caused many people much bewilderment, and has put others off religion altogether.

The *right* answer, I believe, is that what confronts us in these situations is not the character of God but the predicament of man . . . etc. etc.

Or again, suppose that your sermon is setting out to explain that the personal relationshiop with Christ, which is the privilege of every Christian, is not a private but a *shared* relationship within the family of the Church. How do you get quickly into the subject? Here is a suggestion:

Do you play Scrabble? If you do you will have discovered how very much more useful the letter 'E' is than the letter 'I'. Two or three 'E's in your hand offer a welcome variety of usage, but the same number of 'I's are a restrictive embarrassment. Which, when you come to think about it, is very odd because in everyday conversation nothing figures more prominently than the letter

'I'. 'I think.' 'I feel.' 'I like.' *I* – myself as distinct from *you* or *them*.

We normally use the term 'self-centred' to mean 'selfish'. But there is a sense in which we are all self-centred. No one else can think your thoughts, or feel your pain, or experience your pleasure. Inevitably, therefore, we tend to occupy the centre of our little stage, and other people have only the walking-on or walking-off parts. We tend to assume the rightness of our own judgements and to regard ourselves as the standard of normality. How for instance do you conjugate the verb 'to be firm'? 'I am firm. Thou art obstinate. He or she is pig-headed?' Even if in our relations with others we are basically humble and sensitive people, we still inhabit our own world of essentially private thoughts and memories and dreams. And when we come to the great divide of death we must each pass over it alone.

All this is true. But it is not the whole truth. Because we can only be persons in relation to other persons. We depend on other people not only for our food and clothing and all the material things of life . . . etc. etc.

It is hardly necessary to point out that the introduction to the sermon can only be decided when the method of presenting the subject matter has been worked out. The best place from which to start cannot be determined until both the goal of the journey and the particular route chosen to reach it have been selected. It is to this that we must now turn our attention.

2 PRESENTING THE TRUTH—THE BODY OF THE SERMON

As has been said, the preacher's aim is two fold: to make men *see* the truth, and to stimulate them to *want* it for their own possession.

There are, broadly speaking, two methods of approach to the communication of the kind of truths with which we are dealing. There is what the educational text-books call the *deductive* or 'telling' method, and there is the *inductive* or 'revealing' method. It is essential that we should understand their respective functions and use. The difference between the two can be illustrated as follows. Suppose you want a child to know the multiples of two up to, say, twelve. There are two ways by which he may acquire this useful piece of knowledge. He may be made to learn by heart the twice times table. Having got this well into his mind by constant repetition, he can then deduce from this general law its particular application to sweets or marbles. He has been *told* and made to learn the truth in a formula. Its application is a matter of deduction.

Alternatively, the process may be reversed. Let the child be given a dozen bricks with which to experiment for himself. Let him see that if he arranges them in groups of two, there are six; if he arranges them in groups of six, there are two; if he puts them into groups of three, there are four – and so on. Then let him make the same experiments with marbles or oranges, and he will soon come to realize that the same facts apply; that twice six, three fours, and six twos are in every case twelve. He has arrived at the universal truth by a process of induction from particular examples.

Does it matter which method we use? Is one more effective than the other? In the matter of arithmetic perhaps, opinions may differ as between those educationists who incline to the inductive method, and employers who complain that the products of our schools are incapable of accurate mental arithmetic. To this extent, it might seem as if our illustration has been unfortunate. But what is at issue here is not so much a question of the effectiveness of the method employed as that of the aim pursued. It is true that the learning of tables may produce quicker results because it is not necessary to understand numbers in order to do arithmetic. You can know – or rather you can be in possession of the information – that twice six make twelve without ever under-standing why this should be so. But do we want men to learn the truths of the Christian religion in this way? Assuredly not. The concern of the Christian teacher is not simply that men should know the Creed, the Lord's Prayer, and the Church

Catechism *as a formula of words,* but that they should have some real understanding of what these things mean. The truth is more important than the words used to convey it. Anyone who has ever tried to *explain* any matter to somebody else – an electrical or mechanical process maybe – will know the joy of that moment of enlightenment when your would-be pupil sees the point. Most of us also know the sense of paralysis and frustration which descends upon you when he doesn't see the point. He may say politely, 'Yes, I see'. But it's quite obvious that he hasn't seen, and you say to yourself, 'How on earth can I *make* him see?'

Our Lord's task was to make men *see.* How was he to enable them to see the truth in relation to himself and to themselves? To begin by baldly announcing that he was the Messiah would be to invite misunderstanding and to court disaster. In the circumstances of his day the whole idea of the Messiah had become so bound up with nationalist ambitions and the desire for freedom from foreign domination that the very use of the word would be to put a match to a veritable bonfire of misunderstanding. His method, therefore, was to do the works that the prophets had said that Messiah would do, in the hope that people would recognize those actions for what they were. By miracle and parable and story, he appealed to their capacity to see and to recognize the truth for themselves.

It is almost an axiom in teaching that, whenever possible, the best way to teach a truth is to follow the steps by which men have learned it. Now, if we examine the process by which a child acquires the kind of truths that involve recognition – concepts, categories, laws, and principles – we shall find that it is always an inductive process: a building-up from particular examples to the general principle. How, for instance, does a child come to know what a cat is? He sees a small, smooth, black creature with four legs. 'That', says Mummy, 'is a cat.' But the next day he sees a large, smooth black creature, and on inquiry he is told that this also is a 'cat'. Two days later he hears a large, white rough creature with four legs also described as a cat. Gradually, from these and other examples of the cat species, he is able to abstract the idea or principle of 'cat-ness' and thus is enabled to recognise any cat for what it is, irrespective of its size or colour. If anyone doubts that this inductive process is the natural method of learning, let him try teaching a small child what a cat is by inculcating a definition of cat-ness before the child has seen either a cat or a picture of one!

If therefore the preacher is to get his truth across he must proceed inductively, from the particular manifestation(s) or example(s) to the general principle or universal truth. But as we have already argued, the preacher is not concerned simply to secure the intellectual acceptance of his truth. He is anxious that the hearers shall not only *see* the truth but desire it for themselves. The preacher's purpose is not merely to satisfy the mind but to kindle the imagination and arouse desire; not only to communicate Christian truth but to strengthen the hearer's commitment to a relationship with Christ. How can he hope to achieve this?

An illuminating analysis of the process involved is to be found in Ian Ramsey's stimulating book *Religious Language*[1]. The author maintained that what he called a 'religious situation' involves two things, (a) an odd discernment or *disclosure,* revealing more than appears on the surface, and (b) a response or *commitment.* By 'discernment' or 'disclosure' Ramsey meant what we mean when we say 'the penny drops' or 'the situation comes alive'; and by 'response' or 'commitment' the change in attitude or relationship which such a disclosure evokes.

A simple instance will suffice to illustrate this twofold process.

A new couple have moved into a nearby house. No one seems to know who they are, but on the one or two occasions you have exchanged 'Good morning' with the man as you passed on your bicycle, the man's face has seemed vaguely

[1] Published by S.C.M. in 1957. Third impression 1973.

familiar. 'I am sure I have seen that chap before', you say to yourself. 'In Church? No. Some quite different context. But I am blessed if I can remember where. I wonder what kind of job he does that allows him to trim his hedge in the morning.'

Then, one evening you go to a concert given by the nearby City Symphony Orchestra and sit, as you always prefer to do, fairly near the front. Suddenly you realise that the face of the leading ćellist is that of your new neighbour. The penny drops! You say to yourself, 'Of course, I knew I'd seen that chap before, I must make his acquaintence'. You consult the list of players on the back page of the programme to discover his name. There at the head of the ćellos you read 'Michael Meager'. The name rings a bell. 'Meager? Michael Meager? Good Lord, that must be the chap who was Peter's friend at the Royal College. He is about the right age, and anyway there can't be *two* Michael Meagers who play the ćello.'

From being an anonymous neighbour Michael Meager has suddenly become a person to whom you are drawn not only by the common bond of music but also by his friendship with your brother-in-law. In fact you already know quite a bit about him. You know that before becoming a student at the Royal College he had begun reading Law. You know how he met his wife. You know that he is a devotee of Trollope. (Another link with yourself!) You are sure that had Peter still been alive he would most certainly have put you in touch with Michael Meager when he knew that you were both now living in the same town. You decide to make contact with him at the earliest opportunity.

We have all had this kind of experience many times at different levels and in different contexts. Ramsey argued that this two-fold process of *disclosure* followed by a degree of *commitment* is the essence of what he called a 'religious situation'. If this is true, as I believe it is, it is of considerable relevance to the business of preaching. The preacher's task is not to dogmatise but to disclose, to make familiar truth and biblical events 'come alive' in such a way as to stimulate imagination and kindle desire. His job is not to 'hold forth' but to call forth, to evoke response and commitment.

It is relevant to remember that the Gospel we preach is itself a series of disclosure situations. It is the proclamation of things that have happened, of events in which God has acted in relation to men, producing discernment and evoking response. The Christian faith is not a case to be argued but a story to be told. That is why the Bible is the foundation on which all preaching rests. We may or may not preach from a text; our sermons may or may not be expository in nature; but we have no authority other than the truths which God has disclosed in human history and experience, of which the Bible is the sole record.

Let us think of what to many people seems the most theoretical of Christian doctrines – that of the Trinity. What is its origin? Not, as is sometimes supposed, the speculations of theologians, but the experience of practical-minded men. Peter, James, John and the rest were Jews; men born of a race that had clung tenaciously to the conviction that in all the world there is only one God, and that he had chosen them to be his people. For this truth, so greatly at variance with the accepted notions of the rest of the civilized world, their forefathers had fought and died, When Jesus of Nazareth cal11ed them into close association with himself and gradually opened their minds to the truth both that he was Israel's Messiah and also that he stood in a unique relation to God, it did not occur to them that their monotheism was undergoing a considerable revolution. They could but accept the evidence of their senses and the growing conviction of their consciences. After the Resurrection they doubtless found themselves turning to Jesus in their prayers as naturally as they had hitherto turned to God. Even after Pentecost when they began to proclaim boldly that Jesus was both Messiah and Son of God who had poured out his Holy Spirit upon them as he himself had promised and as the prophets had foretold – still they did not concern themselves with the tremendous theological implications of what they were saying. They were not expounders of doctrine; they were primarily witnesses of events and facts. But later on the Church was attacked by critics who said: 'You Christians are extraordinarily inconsistent people. You claim to believe in one God, but in fact you worship two, if not three, Gods. You can't say that Christ is God yet distinct from the Father, and that the Holy Spirit is God yet distinct from them both, and still claim that you believe in *one* God. Do you really mean that there are three Gods, or that God has manifested himself under three different disguises or appearances?'

It was not until she was faced with this kind of challenge that the Church was forced to define her belief in theological terms. But the purpose of the definition was purely preservative. The doctrinal formulae – 'Three in One and One in Three' – 'Of one substance with the Father' – and so on – did not *explain* anything. Still less did they *add* anything. Their purpose was simply to enshrine, in such a way as to avoid ambiguity or misunderstanding, the truth that God had made known to men in the events of history and experience.

The important thing to notice about this process is that it is essentially inductive. It begins with experience and issues in definition, and in this respect the formulation of Christian doctrine has followed the same steps as the discoveries of science. Inevitably so. It is the natural way of learning, and it provides the clue to the best way of teaching and preaching.

When, therefore, we are dealing with any doctrine of the Faith we shall be well advised to proceed inductively. We shall not begin by defining it. To do this is to reverse the natural method of learning. We shall rather try to help our hearers comprehend the truth by entering into the experience of the men to whom God first revealed it. If we use the doctrinal formula at all – and this will largely depend on the purpose of the sermon – we shall use it not as a terminus *a quo* but as a terminus *ad quem*. As such, it may be used either to show how pregnant with experience and significance is the doctrinal language of the Church (which strikes so many people as dry and impersonal because they don't understand its purpose), or we may demonstrate how the particular phrase or statement was, and is intended to be, a safeguard against false interpretations that do violence to the truth as God has revealed it.

I am not laying it down as a rule either that we should never use direct and deductive methods, or that we should never begin with a doctrinal assertion. It is a wise policy occasionally to make a complete change of approach. For example, a Michaelmas sermon might well begin something like this:

> Do you believe in angels? Perhaps you do. So do I. But there are many modern Christians who don't. Some keep an open mind on the subject and would justify themselves by saying that belief in angels is no part of the Creed. Others, more radical, would like to remove all reference to angels from our liturgy and worship on the ground that it's just this kind of unscientific clutter that puts people off the Christian religion.
>
> The fact remains that whether we like it or not there's a good deal in the Bible about angels . . . etc. etc.

What matters is not that we should never begin by plunging in at the deep end, but that the movement of thought in the sermon as a whole should follow the natural method of learning, moving inductively from the particular example to the general truth, not vice versa. It is inevitable that a great deal of our preaching must make reference to truths the foundations of which it would be impossible to explain every time they are mentioned. Again, many sermons will take the form of a discussion between preacher and congregation, in which he will voice the kind of thoughts or questions that his statements are likely to produce in their minds. Question and answer, point and counter point, will be directed towards elucidation in the Socratic manner. Such a method doubtless contains deductive elements, but its overriding purpose is inductive because its concern is that men shall see for themselves the truth and its relevance. Too many sermons are little more than mere assertion without either explanation or the orderly arrangement of facts. We shall not expatiate on the love of God, we shall show it in action. We shall not analyse a doctrinal formula, we shall help men to grasp for themselves the truth that the formula preserves. We shall not deal with truth in the abstract, but in the concrete situations of daily life. Our task is not to indoctrinate men, but to help them to see for themselves the truth as it is in Christ.

We shall discuss the need and use of illustrations in a later chapter, but this is a convenient point at which to utter a brief warning against the danger of abstraction. Many of us are apt in our preaching to be far too abstract. Our training has made us capable of conceptual thinking. But it is a facility that our people, for the most part, do not share, and when we indulge in it from the pulpit, they find themselves out of their depth. The fact that the whole universe is God's creation and therefore (apart from sin) consistent, means that God's revelations of himself in history are congruous with (though they go far beyond) the expression of his purpose in the created order. Hence, while in experience men have come to know a truth by a process of induction, they may come more clearly to comprehend it by reflection, comparison, and analogy. To return to the doctrine of the Trinity: the process by which the Church came to hold it was inductive. But we may be helped more fully to understand it by an analogy such as that drawn from the experience of the creative artist by Miss Dorothy L. Sayers in her stimulating book *The Mind of the Maker.* The purpose of this kind of analogy, however, is to illuminate the truth, not to establish it. Men have not come to believe that God is a Trinity of Father, Son, and Holy Spirit, because the processes of creative art involve three such stages or phases. But, given, on other grounds, the Trinitarian doctrine on God, the analogous experience of the creative artist is immensely illuminating. The use of such illustrations is an essential part of the preacher's art, and one that should be developed by constant practice. When the truth has been presented inductively it may often be further illuminated by analogy.

So far we have tried to make clear that the first step in the process of communication is that of making contact with the mind of the hearer, helping him actively to welcome and receive the truth to be presented. The second step is the presentation of the newcomer. The more unfamiliar this guest is, the more necessary it is for him to accommodate his speech and behaviour to that of his host. He must be careful to observe the manners and customs of his new home. In other words, the preacher must present his truth in a manner that is native and natural to the minds of his hearers, not in some forced or formal dress that may be familiar to him but strange to them.

3 APPLICATION TO LIFE

The third principle or stage is self-evident, it is spelling out the reason or purpose you have in preaching the sermon. It is the 'because' of having said to yourself, 'I want to preach about Peter's denial *because. . . .*' It is the point at which all that was said on pp. 21–31 is translated into terms of everyday Christian living. Your AIM is made clear in the APPLICATION.

The preacher's function is not that of handing out Christian knowledge and information, however stimulating and valuable. His duty is to assist men in the actual living of the Christian life. To this end, knowledge of our Lord's life, of the biblical history of man's redemption, together with some grasp of the meaning of these events in terms of authentic Christian belief, is essential. But it is not by itself enough. 'So what?' is the question that the man in the pew has every right to ask of the man in the pulpit at the conclusion of his presentation. 'What does all this that you have said mean in practice? How does it affect me? What ought I to do about it?'

The Christian ethic, we are told, cannot be divorced from the Christian dogma. Neither should Christian dogma be presented in isolation from the Christian ethic. What distinguished the religion of Israel was (among other things) the refusal of Israel's spiritual pastors to allow religion to become separated from morality. 'Ye shall be holy, for I am holy', said the Lord. Justice and mercy, no less than sacrifice and observance, were required of men because God was a God of righteousness. It is no less so for the Christian. Yet much of the ignorance of the people of this nation about the Christian faith is not the result of their never having been taught, but of their not having been made to see any connection between their Scripture lessons and their daily lives. There is no Christian doctrine but calls forth an appropriate devotion, and carries with it a corresponding duty. It is the preacher's concern that these shall not be allowed to exist in isolation from each other. To each truth there is attached a *so* or *therefore*: I believe in God the Father, Maker of heaven and earth – *therefore* I am responsible to God for my use of the creatures he has made. I may not use any other person, man or woman, boy or girl, merely to give me pleasure or satisfaction. I am not free to do whatever I like with the 'raw materials' of Nature. My use of them must be governed by the purpose for which God has given them, and by my duty to keep his commandments. Just as no moral question can be answered except in terms of what we believe about God and his purpose, so what we believe about God carries corresponding moral obligations. What is called the Christian 'attitude' to sex and marriage, for example, is not the exhibition of an old-fashioned prudery; it is the inescapable logic of what Christians believe about God's purpose in creating and redeeming men and women.

The third function of the preaching process therefore is answering the question 'So what?' Yet although this function has, for convenience, been called the 'application', it must not be thought of as a final coming down to earth of something that has hitherto been in the air. Enough has already been said about the dangers of abstraction and the need for concreteness of presentation to stress the fact that, unless the moral and practical relevance of the sermon has been to some degree apparent throughout, the hearer's attention may well have been lost long before the application is reached.

In many sermons the application will be so obviously implicit in what has been said that there is little need to stress it further, save perhaps to underline it in one or two short sentences. Other sermons, especially those which have been presented in terms of some biblical incident or character, may need a more extended application to present-day circumstances. Or, again, the preacher may wish to direct to some particular aspect a sermon, the general practical bearing of which is already quite clear. Sometimes the best method of application is to let the members of the congregation make it themselves in the prayer after the sermon. But whether the application be a clearly marked third stage or whether it emerges inescapably in the course of the presentation, the sermon must be brought to a point and finish on a positive and unambiguous note. It should not, as some sermons do, simply fizzle out.

It may be that the preacher has been dealing with some foundation doctrine from which a number of different duties arise, and to which a variety of devotional responses – praise, thanksgiving, penitence – are all equally appropriate. But it is to be hoped that, having written the bulk of his sermon, he is not left speculating about the best note on which to conclude it. That decision should have been made as part of the process of defining his aim. If he is undecided about the point to which he proposes to lead his sermon, he is almost bound to introduce what afterwards prove to be irrelevancies, and to leave a number of loose ends. It does sometimes happen – as most preachers of experience will testify – that, in the process of writing out, the sermon takes charge of the writer and instists on following a different line of thought from that which the preacher intended! This is because another thought train that had been going on just below the level of consciousness, or, as we say, 'at the back of his mind', has suddenly forced its way to the front and taken charge of the preacher's thinking. When this happens it is usually because this usurping line of development is a better one, or is more satisfying to the preacher than the one with which he started. Subjectively, the process seems like inspiration (and who would deny that it is?). But when the inspiration has worked itself out it is usually wise to examine it objectively to ensure that it will appear as clear and compelling to the hearer as its writing has seemed to the preacher.

In all this that we have said about the introduction and the application of the sermon our Lord is our model. He begins with his hearer's everyday experience: 'What man of you, having a hundred sheep, if he has lost one of them, does not leave the ninety-nine in the wilderness, and go after the one which is lost, until he finds it? . . . Even so, I tell you, there will be more joy in heaven over one sinner who repents than over ninety-nine righteous persons who need no repentance.' (Luke 15.4–7) 'At that time, tax collections and other bad characters were all crowding in to listen to him; and the Pharisees and the doctors of the law began grumbling among themselves: ''This fellow,'' they said, ''welcomes sinners and eats with them''.Jesus answered them with this parable. . . .' (Luke 15. 1–3) 'A man in the crowd said to him, ''Master, tell my brother to divide the family property with me. . . .''' (Luke 12.13). Definite questions. Live issues. Immediate situations. Religion related to daily life.

The three principles we have considered are simply a description of the process of communication as they apply to the preacher. The three things he must do – Register, Reveal, Relate – determine the shape of the sermon. Thus:

First: INTRODUCTION – preparing the mind to receive the truth.

Second: PRESENTATION of the truth in such a way that the hearer can assimilate it.

Third: APPLICATION of the truth to daily Christian living.

This shape is not an ecclesiastical tradition or an artistic convention. It is essentially utilitarian. It is determined by what the sermon is designed to do. I recall Dr. Donald Coggan when Archbishop of York saying in a lecture on preaching (I am quoting from memory) 'Many of the sermons I hear need a pair of corsets. They have no form or comeliness and when we hear them there is no beauty that we desire of them.'

It is important to note that this is not what used to be called 'the Rule of Three'. It is quite true that 'a sermon should have, as Aristotle long ago told us, a beginning, a middle, and an end', and that 'the rule of three is a principle of thought also. The sentence has a subject, a predicate, and usually an object. . . .'[1] But this does *not* mean, as very many theological students have been taught, that a sermon should make three points. Generally speaking, a sermon should have only one point, and deal with only one truth. But this truth will pass through three stages. A Methodist lay preacher whose simple sermons were much appreciated by the congregation in his circuit was once asked the secret of his success. 'Well,' he answered, 'first, I tells 'em what I'm going to tell 'em; then I tells 'em; then I tells 'em what I've told 'em.' The sooner we break away from the inherited tradition of a parsonic trinity of points and learn to deal with only one thing per sermon, the less confused and the better instructed our people will be. There is a natural trinity about a sermon, but it should be a trinity of structure not of points. One truth – three stages – that is the psychology of the matter.

If it be argued that there are some subjects that have two or three different aspects, then deal with them in two or three sermons. For example, the subject of sin could be dealt with in terms of the world, the flesh and the devil. Don't attempt to deal with them all at once. Simplicity in a sermon is not to be confused with baldness and bareness. You may have a variety of illustrations; you may even deal with your subject from different aspects – so long as you are all the time dealing with one truth and are presenting that truth with a single aim. It would be absurd to suggest that this rule should never in any circumstances be broken. There are doubtless some subjects and some occasions that permit of the attempt to say more than one thing at a time. But the preacher will be the better able to make good use of these occasional departures if he normally practises the restraint of only trying to say one

[1] Charles Smyth, *The Art of Preaching* p. 48

thing per sermon, and has acquired some skill in the art of saying it effectively.

Our three principles, then, determine the structure of the sermon because they represent the three necessary steps in the communication and assimilation of a truth. But it does not in the least follow that the three steps shall be of even approximately the same length. Clearly the bulk of the sermon will be occupied with the presentation. The introduction may be quite brief, or it may require several minutes. Similarly, the relating to life, or application, may require a reasonably full explanation, or it may need no more than three of our sentences. Incidentally, it makes for a sense of artistic unity if in this final section the preacher is able to refer, however briefly, to the line of thought or illustration with which the sermon began. But the process is not complete without all three stages.

Further, it will be apparent that the three stages of the sermon, as they ultimately take shape in the final result, will be in reverse order from that in which the preacher first thought them out. What first comes to the ears of the hearer – the introduction – will have come last to the mind of the preacher, since he cannot select his starting point until he has determined both the goal at which he is aiming and the route by which he hopes to reach it.

Chapter 5

The Principles in Practice: Planning the Sermon

Let us now apply our three principles to the planning of a sermon.

It has already been argued[1] that no sermon can properly be thought out until the preacher has defined his aim; until, in other words, he knows why he wants to preach it.

Sometimes he will be conscious of his aim before he selects his subject-matter. He desires to teach a particular truth or to correct a common misunderstanding. That is his aim. He must then consider by what means and using what material he can best achieve it. Such a desire often arises in the course of pastoral work. For instance, a remark made to him after a funeral may reveal how very un-Christian are many of the current notions concerning death. From reflection on this fact is born a desire to give more explicit teaching about it from the pulpit. 'I want', he says to himself, 'to correct the false notions of death that are really based on pagan ideas about the immortality of the soul, and to make clear that the Christian doctrine of death is that it is something that must be

[1] See p. 35

57

voluntarily accepted before we can enjoy the fruits of the Resurrection.' This is a fairly comprehensive aim, and the preacher must then ask himself, 'Can I do this in one sermon? Is there not so much involved here – the idea of survival, the meaning of our Lord's Resurrection, the connection of death with sin, etc. – that I shall need three or possibly four sermons to deal with it properly? Suppose I attempted it in one sermon, how should I set about it? Can I base it on some parable, for example, Dives and Lazarus, or the text, "Except a grain of wheat fall into the earth and die, it abideth alone . . ."? Or would it be better to explain that the Apostles who burst upon the world with the good news of Jesus and the Resurrection were men who never had any doubts about personal survival; men who in some sense believed in a resurrection before ever they met Jesus? It would then be possible, by contrasting the earlier Hebrew notion of Sheol with the later idea of resurrection, to make clear that a completely new light was shed on these ideas by the Resurrection of Christ. How much needs to be said about the connection between death and sin? Can I make use of St Paul's well-known words, "As in Adam all die, even so in Christ shall all be made alive"?' After such reflection the preacher may decide that the subject is altogether too vast for one sermon. So he plans to make three sermons of it, basing each of them on the kind of text or statement that is apt to be quoted on gravestones:

1 Rest in Peace.
2 Alive unto God.
3 Death is swallowed up in victory.

Conversely – and probably more often – it is a particular subject that first comes to the mind, and we have then to decide to what purpose we will put it. This often happens when the subject is provided by the Christian Calendar. 'Sunday evening is the first Evensong of St Barnabas, and I ought therefore to preach about him. What shall I say?'

Here is a situation so common that it may be worth thinking out in some detail. The first question to ask is: In what way is St Barnabas specially relevant to the present life of the congregation? At this stage the preacher will be well advised to jot down a few facts about St Barnabas, and see what they suggest. Thus:

Facts	*Suggestions*
(a) Barnabas – son of consolation.	The patron saint of nurses. Hospitals? Ministry of healing – spiritual and physical?
(b) 'A good man, full of the Holy Ghost and of faith.'	What place does natural goodness occupy in the Christian life?
(c) He sold a field and gave the price of it to the Apostles.	Free-will offering. Can this first enthusiastic sharing-out of funds among the first Christians in Jerusalem have any equivalent among members of a congregation today? Should it?
(d) Barnabas's championship of St Paul.	Would St Paul ever have been accepted as a fellow-worker by the Church had it not been for the mediation of Barnabas? In what ways can Christians act in this mediating and reconciling role today?
(e) The dispute about St Mark.	It's salutary to be reminded that even the Apostles didn't always agree. How did they deal with their differences? In this case they agreed to differ. Why? Presumably because no fundamental principle was at stake. What did they do when such principles *were* at stake? For example, the question of the admission of Gentile converts? 'It seemed good to the Holy Ghost and to us.' Do we sufficiently distinguish between differences of opinion and differen-

ces of principle? And how should we deal (within the congregation) with each kind of difference? Parish Meeting? Prayer groups? Putting it to the vote?

This last is clearly a fruitful theme, and one very relevant to the present life of the congregation. However, let us just review the other four, and make sure that there is not something of even prior importance. (b) is possible. (c) was dealt with in a course on 'Christian Giving' a few months ago. (e) is the most closely related to our present stage of development. The aim is already clear – 'To show how necessary it is to distinguish between differences of mere opinion from those of principle, as illustrated by the story of Barnabas and Paul; and how we should try to deal with them in our personal and congregational life.'

The subject-matter of the sermon has been chosen in the selection of our aim – the dispute between Paul and Barnabas about John Mark. How is it to be presented? Obviously by narrative. How can it be made more vivid? Is there any part of the story as told in the Acts that needs a bit of filling out? Yes, the actual argument between the two apostles. It is not difficult to imagine the kind of arguments each would use – 'You're being too hard on the lad'. 'Maybe, but in a matter of this kind one can't afford to be soft, etc., etc.' Incidentally, it will provide a useful illustration of the need, when reading the Bible, of entering imaginatively into the situation.[1] Will this suffice to make the point? It might, if I were only trying to distinguish between differences of opinion and those of principle. But I really want to show the need for trying to deal with the latter by prayer. In which case I must draw the contrast with, for example, the Council of Jerusalem. Is this going to be too much for one sermon? It might. I had better see how it works out.

---

[1] See p. 121

Now, what about the introduction? Well, what is the line along which I want to get them thinking? Differences – of opinion and of principle (and of clashes of self-interest?) and the need for a common purpose. There should be plenty of everyday examples of these. Oh, what was that I heard the other day about the Pearsons – 'never had a cross word'. Can two people live together without differences of opinion? At any rate, here is a line of approach. Let us see how it works out.

INTRODUCTION

'Never had a cross word in twenty-five years.' Does this mean no bad tempers or no differences of opinion? The inevitability of differences of opinion and desire, and the need for a common purpose. For example, in marriage and in other common enterprises. An excellent illustration of this is provided by:

PRESENTATION

Barnabas (feast tomorrow) and Paul. Two men of quite different types of character.

The story of Barnabas's championship of Paul, and of the first missionary journey. Mark returns – homesick and seasick.

The question later raised by Barnabas. The argument:

B.: 'You're too hard on the lad.'

P.: 'We can't take chances. The work is too important.'

B.: 'Our Lord would have given him a second chance. What about Peter?'

P.: 'Possibly. But I can't take the responsibility.'

Who was right? It doesn't matter basically, because each was determined that the *work* should go on.

Suppose the difference had been one of principle?

They would have had to resolve it by prayer. Compare the Gentile Christians and the Council of Jerusalem.

CONCLUSION

So with us. In our personal relationships with others we must try to distinguish between differences that are merely temperamental, and differences of principle and purpose. In our church life we should learn to accept charitably these purely personal differences. But matters of truth and principle must be settled, not by majority vote, but by prayer.

There is the sermon. To write it out in full is now comparatively simple. (For the stage shown above most preachers develop their own shorthand and contractions.) The aim, the beginning, the line of development, and the conclusion are now clearly seen in the preacher's mind. The rest is just a matter of pruning and polishing. However, on the assumption that the sermon is to be written out in full, let us now write it.

ST BARNABAS

I was hearing the other day of a couple who in twenty-five years of married life claimed never to have had a cross word. I don't quite know what a statement like that is intended to mean. If it means that, whatever their differences of opinion, they never got heated and said hard things, that would be altogether lovely. But if it means that they never *had* any differences of opinion, then it sounds to me very much like the marriage of a couple of jellyfish!

For clashes of opinion will arise in the best-regulated households: clashes that are entirely legitimate. They arise partly from differences of temperament, and partly from the fact that no one of us can know the whole truth about anything. What matters about human relations in general, and marriage in particular, is that men and women should be *aiming at the same goal,* and acknowledging a common authority outside the circle of their own immediate interests. Differences of temperament and opinion will then add a certain amount of sparkle, but they won't give rise to quarrels.

What is called in the divorce court 'incompatibility of temperament' is really nothing of the kind. It's a good thing that husband and wife should *not* be of the same temperament. The trouble arises when each has a different conception of the purpose for which their marriage exists. If one wants to spend every evening at home, and the other wants to spend every evening out, if one wants to have children, and the other doesn't; if one thinks of love as self-sacrifice and the other thinks of it as self-satisfaction – that's when the trouble starts! Indeed, unless two people have the same idea of what marriage is, and of what they should be aiming at in their marriage, they never ought to marry at all. So long as they have the same basic values and the same overriding purpose, their differences and temperament won't in the least weaken their real and permanent relationship. In unimportant matters they can agree to differ (and these differences can be a source of amusement). In a matter of real importance they must either work it out together or one must grant to the other the right to exercise a casting vote.

That is true not only of marriage but of all sorts of human relationships. A real breach only occurs when men are seeking different ends, as in the clashes between capital and labour, or as between the conflicting interests of one group of men *versus* another. It's only when men are seeking the same ultimate goal, serving the same overriding purpose, that they can work together happily despite their differences, and, as we say, agree to differ.

A very good illustration of this is provided by the celebrated clash, recorded in the Acts of the Apostles, between Paul and Barnabas. Here were two men of very different temperament.

St Paul, as we all know, was the kind of man who never did anything by halves. When he was a Pharisee he was an uncompromising Pharisee, and when he became a Christian he was an uncompromising Christian. He didn't suffer fools gladly, and he found it very hard to bear patiently with people who did not see eye to eye with himself. It was these very qualities that made him such an effective apostle, but must have made him very difficult to live with.

Barnabas was a man of very different stamp. The name 'Barnabas' means 'the son of consolation', and when he first appears in the pages of the Acts he is described as 'a good man, full of the Holy Ghost and of faith'. Indeed, it was Barnabas who first persuaded the Church to accept Paul as a fellow worker. The truth is that, though they had no doubt of the genuineness of his conversion, the disciples were a little scared of Paul. He was a bit too much of a firebrand for their liking and, quite frankly, they didn't know what to do with him. However, hearing that some of the brethren had been making converts in Antioch, the Church in Jerusalem decided to send Barnabas to shepherd and instruct these new Christians, and the first thing Barnabas did was to seek out Paul (who had been kicking his heels in Tarsus) and to invite his help. It was not till then that St Paul, as the protégé of Barnabas, was really accepted by the Church, and the two men formed a spiritual partnership of which Paul very quickly became the leader.

So it was, that, having proved their worth at Antioch, these two men were chosen to undertake the first missionary expedition into Asia Minor, and it was then that Paul's great gifts of leadership and his indomitable courage came to the fore.

So they set off on their great adventure, taking with them (presumably at the suggestion of Barnabas) his young nephew, John Mark, to be a kind of batman and apprentice. Though probably still in his 'teens, Mark had been a disciple of our Lord in Jerusalem, and we can imagine with what enthusiasm he accepted the invitation to share in the first missionary adventure with his uncle.

But we can also easily imagine that he found it all very much harder going than he anticipated. His first taste of the sea probably made him very sick; the pace of work and travel set by St Paul was very hard to keep; and the Gentile cities of the Mediterranean seaboard seemed very strange and foreign after his home city of Jerusalem. Anyhow, it wasn't very long before he became so homesick that he felt he couldn't go on any farther, and he asked leave to go back home.

It was probably just as well for him that he did, for it wasn't till after Mark had left them that the two Apostles ran into serious trouble, encountering fierce Jewish opposition, street fighting, stone throwing, and what not.

However, so far as Mark was concerned, the incident was closed, and might have remained so, if, when a second expedition was proposed, Barnabas had not suggested that Mark should again be asked to go with them. 'But,' says the Acts, 'Paul thought it not good to take him with them who had departed from them in Pamphylia, and went not with them to the work.' So there arose a sharp difference of opinion between the two Apostles and neither would give way. You can almost hear them arguing:

'Oh, come,' says Barnabas, 'have a heart. The lad was only sixteen, and he'd never been away from home before. I think it's very natural that he should get homesick on his first trip out. But he's older now, and he knows what he's in for.'

'That's all very well,' says Paul. 'You're only thinking of your nephew. I'm thinking about the work of spreading the Gospel, and that's so vital that we can't afford to take any chances with doubtful starters. You may remember that our Lord said that "no man, having put his hand to the plough, and looking back is fit for the Kingdom of God". Well, young Mark did look back. I know he's young, and I know he's a loyal disciple, but he isn't of the stuff that's going to carry the Gospel into Asia.'

'But, my dear Paul, you can't judge a man's whole future by the mistakes he makes when he's sixteen. Even Peter denied our Lord once, you know, and he was a good deal older than John. I must say I think you're being a bit hard.'

'Yes,' says Paul, 'maybe. But in a matter of this kind we can't afford to be soft, either with ourselves or anybody else. . . .'

So the argument went on: Paul with his strong sense of the demands of the Kingdom being a bit rigorist and unyielding; Barnabas (truly called the son of consolation) pleading for the more generous view. But as neither would give way, they agreed to differ and parted company. Barnabas took Mark and went off to Cyprus, and Paul found a new partner in Silas.

Well, which of them was right, do you think? It's difficult

to say. They were probably both right. At least you couldn't say that either of them was wrong! Considered purely as a question of the proper treatment of John Mark, Barnabas was undoubtedly right. But having regard to the larger question of spreading the Gospel, Paul was probably right in insisting that to rely on Mark was a risk that he, at any rate, did not feel it right to take.

The difference between the two men was largely a difference of temperament and mental make-up, and it wasn't a matter of any vital moment. It's not as if either of them was going to throw up the work because they didn't agree. It wouldn't seriously affect the spread of the Gospel whether Paul and Barnabas worked together or whether each of them had a different partner, because – and this is the point – both of them were entirely at one in their overriding desire to serve our Lord and to further his Kingdom, and each of them knew that to be true of the other. So they could agree to differ, and remain firm friends.

Had the difference between them been one of *principle,* then they would have had to resolve it by prayer; praying about it and thinking about it until they had arrived at what seemed to be God's will in the matter.

Such a problem and such a way of tackling it had already arisen in their experience. Their first mission into Asia Minor had gained a considerable number of converts from among the Gentile races. To many Jewish Christians this seemed a by-passing, almost a denial, of all that God had done in and for his Chosen People; and they claimed that if non-Jews were to be admitted to the Church they must be made to keep the Jewish law. To others, and to Paul and Barnabas especially, it was clear that any such condition would erect an impossible barrier to the acceptance of the Gospel by the Gentile nations. Here, indeed, was a difference of principle; an issue on which the whole future of the Church depended.

So Paul and Barnabas went to Jerusalem to lay the whole matter before the elders of the Church. Each side presented its case and submitted it in prayer to God. They prayed that he would show them his will, and they went on thinking and praying, praying and thinking, until they had reached a common mind. Indeed, so convinced were they that this common mind was the mind of Christ, that in declaring their conclusion they said, 'It seemed good to the Holy Ghost and to us . . .'.

In these two incidents we can see, I believe, the principles that are involved in our relationships with other people, and especially with our fellow Christians.

In all our dealings with others we must try to distinguish between differences that are really differences of conviction and purpose, and those that are merely temperamental. About these latter we can, and should, agree to differ, recognizing that no human opinion is infallible, and that one is just as likely to be right (or wrong) as the other.

Where the clash is one of principle and purpose, as for example between the Christian and the secular way of life, then we must hold fast to our principles, while trying to be as charitable as possible towards persons.

In the life of the Church – in our own parish family, for example – we must recognize that we are not all cast in the same mould. The Church is made up of all kinds of people and it needs all kinds. We need those who have Paul's uncompromising devotion to our Lord, and we need those with the unquenchable generosity of Barnabas. But we must distinguish between the differences of judgement and opinion that are bound to arise from our varied temperaments, and those that are really matters of principle. We can settle the first kind by friendly discussion and, possibly a majority vote. But in the deeper and more important matters that affect the spiritual life of the congregation we must not attempt to settle things by mere argument and voting. We must learn to wait on God in prayer, and to go on praying and thinking and praying until we have reached the sort of common mind of which we can say, 'It seems good to the Holy Spirit and to us . . .'.

*   *   *

Well, there it is. It will need a bit of polishing and pruning (for example, have the words 'difference' and 'principle' been used rather too often?), but this can be done as we read it through several times before preaching it.

It will be quite clear that this sermon has raised an issue – that of trying to discover the mind of the Holy Ghost for the Church – that requires further explanation. One sermon often necessitates two or three others. In this case the parish priest must decide just how much further, and to what immediate parochial application, he wants to lead his people's thoughts. If, for instance, he is working towards a parish meeting, or if there is some important matter coming up for decision in the parish, here is his chance to press the point home with a further sermon about how the early Church seemed to live under the constant guidance of the Holy Spirit, and how we must seek to do the same. Here a further question arises: 'If I follow this up immediately, will it mean altering my preaching plans for the next few Sundays? Well, Sunday week there'll be John the Baptist, and then St Peter. That leaves next Sunday clear for following up this matter of prayer. If I find that I need more than one other sermon, I shall have to see what can be done about bringing John the Baptist into the picture.'

It may be argued that the process of arriving at this sermon has been simplified over-much; that in practice a preacher often spends more time than is here indicated in following up the possibilities presented by one or more of the first five suggestions. He may even get to the length of planning three-quarters of a sermon and then decide to scrap it because it is not 'coming right' or saying what he really wants to say. This is true, but it is largely a matter of practice. The young preacher will be well advised to jot down all the various possibilities of a subject that occur to him. After a year or two he will probably find that he can accomplish this preliminary work of selection with a bare minimum of writing, or even with none at all. When his aim has been determined he will then have to consider:

1. Subject-matter and method of presentation.
2. The point to which he intends to bring it, and the

manner of its expression (that is, in general or particular terms).

3. The line of introduction that will link his theme with his hearers' present knowledge and get their minds moving in the direction along which he wants to lead them further.

Sometimes his aim and subject-matter will come simultaneously to mind because they are clearly inseparable. 'I want to preach about our Lord's miracles. Why? Because I want to make clear that they were not done to attract attention, but as the "works of Messiah".'

At other times his aim will present a quite bewildering array of possibilities. Take, for example, the aim, 'To show that "faith" is not simply believing something with your mind, but doing something with your life on the basis of your belief'. Almost any of the great characters of the Bible could be used to illustrate this truth – Abraham, Moses, Elijah, David, Jeremiah, or any one of the Apostles. The method of presentation would then be mainly narrative. Alternatively, the preacher may be so concerned to sort out the modern misunderstandings about the nature of faith that he devotes the whole of his address to distinguishing belief as a function of the mind, from faith considered as an act of will and trust, showing the relation between the two and illustrating his argument from everyday life. The choice before him here is not between different goals, but between different routes to a goal already determined. It is hard to resist the temptation to 'rub it in' by adding – his job is to ensure to the best of his ability that he does not make his journey alone, or accompanied by a few stragglers, but that he takes the whole of his congregation with him!

Chapter 6

The Tools and Skills of The Preacher's Craft

The sermon on St Barnabas described in the previous chapter was a very simple straightforward exercise, making no special demands on the preacher's originality or skill. It was provided simply to illustrate the shaping of a sermon and the mental processes by which it is reached. There are, however, many sermons of a very different type from this, other ways of presentation, other devices and skills of which the preacher must learn to make use. In this chapter we shall consider the more important of these, having in mind not so much the introduction or application but the main body or presentation of the sermon.

At this stage it will be as well to remind ourselves once more that the purpose of the sermon is not that it should be remembered, but that it should be received. The preacher's task is to convince men of the truth and to convict them by it, not as the logical end of a chain of reasoning but because they have been made to *see* it, and in seeing to desire it. If I want to persuade my friend, who has never been north of York, to take his holiday in Galloway, I do not begin by showing him a map. I show him photographs of lovely scenes, and try to fire his imagination by telling him of the beauty, the romance, and the historical associations of Kirkcudbrightshire. When his interest has been aroused, out comes the map, and we begin to discuss how to get there and where to stay. The preacher's procedure is not dissimilar. He is persuading men to penetrate what to the natural man is an unfamiliar realm and to experience its richness for themselves. If he fails to help them in some measure to see its scenery, to sense its atmosphere and to desire it for themselves, there will be little point in his issuing instructions on how to get there. Yet to see a thing is not necessarily to desire it. It all depends on the thing seen, and on the scale of values of the observer. The Christian preacher has at least the assurance that, though men may not desire the truth of God, there is nothing better that he or anyone else can show them. The chances of men wanting it when they see it will depend not so much on his powers of persuasion, as on his ability to make them *see,* though the way in which he does it and his own obvious love of it may go far to influence their response.

1   CONTRASTS AND CONJECTURES

Many, perhaps the majority, of sermons are cast in the form of a dialogue or discussion. The preacher begins with an incident or a proposition and 'discusses' it – sometimes in the form of question and answer, sometimes as a kind of debate in which he tries fairly to express the doubts and difficulties that exist in the minds of many people. The danger to which this method is exposed is that of reducing the sermon to the level of mere argument and assertion, appealing only to the reason and ignoring the more important elements of the imagination and desire. It is to enable the preacher to effect *disclosure* and evoke *commitment* that he must make frequent use of these other tools and skills with which we are here concerned.

The step by step argument is by no means the only effective method of presentation. There are others which the preacher can often use with greater effect. One is the use of contrasts. There are contrasts of character or circumstance which can often bring to life the truth with which the preacher is concerned, e.g. Martha and Mary, the vigorous Saul and gentle Barnabas, the impulsiveness of Peter and the caution of Thomas. There is Amos the simple shepherd shouting his indignation in the market-place (and being moved on by the police) and Isaiah the aristrocat, moving in court circles, expressing the same truth in matchless poetry.

Then there are contrasts of ideas – 'the secular *versus* the Christian' – which lend themselves readily to such subjects as the secular *versus* the Christian doctrine of man, the Christian *versus* the secular view of history, the Christian *versus* the secular understanding of the purpose of the human life, the Christian *versus* the secular use of material possessions and so on. Sometimes there are more than two possible alternatives, e.g. the three possible views about the purpose of human life and history, 'the optimistic, the pessimistic or the Christian'.

Another useful device is what might be called the 'What if not?' – What if the Jews had not rejected Jesus as their Messiah? (i.e. how would this have affected the entry of the Gentiles into the New Covenant?) What if Jesus had not been prepared to face the Cross? What if Peter had rushed out after his denial and like Judas killed himself? Suppose Paul had been persuaded by his friends *not* to go to Jerusalem and suffer imprisonment in consequence? Did he make the right decision? What if Jeremiah had chosen to accept the offer to go with his fellow Jews to Babylon? Did he make the right decision? If not, can God use our wrong decisions if made from the highest motives?

2   ILLUSTRATIONS

Simple people tend to think in pictures and in very concrete terms. The ability to think in terms of principles and abstractions is possible only to certain types of mind, and even then only as the result of training. This is a fact that we clergy are apt to forget, and our preaching is often far too abstract for many of our hearers. It is of little use to cultivate the art of speaking to our people in their own language, if we ask them to follow us in processes of thought with which they are largely unfamiliar. We shall only enable our hearers to grasp eternal verities if we present them in terms of familiar home-truths.

You are taking the adult confirmation class. The subject under discussion is prayer, and you are trying to make clear the need to begin prayer by recollecting the presence of God. John immediately raises a question, 'But aren't you just creating God out of your own imagination?' You reply, 'Oh no, you are not thinking God into existence. He is there already. All you are doing is trying to realise the fact'. John still looks puzzled. So you say, 'Tell me John, have you a radio at home?' 'Yes, three as a matter of fact' 'Right. Now when you go home and turn on the radio and fill your room with music, what has happened? Your radio set has not created the music. All you have done is to fulfil the electronic conditions necessary for making what we might call in these days of twenty-four hour broadcasting, that "ever present music" a reality for you. You have simply "tuned-in" to what is already there.' 'Ah,' says John, 'I see'? Light dawns.The penny drops. You have used a fact which is within his experience to illuminate something which was hitherto outside it.

Here, as in all else, the preacher's model is our Lord himself. Consider the question put to him by the lawyer, 'Who is my neighbour?' Jesus could have replied, 'Your neighbour, my friend, is anyone whom you encounter in everday life and whose need makes some demand on your compassion' – a reply that would have left the lawyer exactly where he was before. Instead, our Lord told the story of the Good Samaritan and pressed home the point by making the 'neighbour' not a fellow Jew but a hated Samaritan. Jesus rarely enunciated a principle except to clinch a point that he had already made transparently clear in one or more telling illustrations drawn from the everyday life and experience of those to whom he spoke. Indeed, with such a precedent, it is astonishing that there should ever have been a time when illustrations were regarded with disfavour by Christian preachers.

Few today would question the necessity of their use. Illustrations and example are not an artistic adornment, they are a way of 'getting over'. They are but an application of the inductive movement of thought – from particular cases to the general concept. Not all preachers have the type of mind to which illustrations come easily, and some make this an excuse for not using them in their preaching. Where this is the case the art of illustration should be – and can be – deliberately cultivated. I have myself made it a systematic practice for many years to supply my own illustrations when reading a theological book. 'Suppose I were trying to teach this truth to others; how would I illustrate it? What is the point or principle involved? What is analogous to it in everday experience?' It has been an exacting but immensely profitable discipline. But it has been done, let me add, not primarily to improve my preaching but to deepen my understanding of what I am reading; the assumption being that *if I can't produce an illustration, it's because I haven't properly understood the point at issue.*

3   THE USE OF NARRATIVE AND STORY

There is probably no part of the preacher's art that has been so neglected as the use of narrative and stories, and certainly there is no method of presentation that has greater potential power. Stories are older than literature; everyone loves a tale. Notice how in any company ears are pricked up when somebody says, 'Have you heard the story about . . .?' My experience of clerical gatherings is that most clerics are good raconteurs, and it is a thousand pities that so few of us put our skill in story-telling to good account in the pulpit. I don't suggest that we should follow the example of those preachers whose sermons seem to consist largely of a loosely connected string of anecdote and reminiscence. Few things are more enervating. If we are to use the story medium we must know not only how to tell a story but why we are telling it. The effectiveness of our use of the narrative method will largely depend on our understanding of its psychology.

Basically, the function of the story (for the purpose of the preacher and teacher) is to help men to see a truth more clearly and compellingly than they are likely to see it in any other way. In its simplest use the story is a dramatized illustration. A truth or principle that might be tedious or hard to grasp if presented in general or abstract terms is made clear by being cast in the concrete, dramatized form of a story. 'Truth embodied in a tale can enter in at lowly doors.' You wish, for example, to preach a sermon about divorce. If you begin:

'To-night, I want you to think about one of the greatest evils of our time; one that has probably caused more suffering and heartbreak than any other. I am referring, of course, to divorce . . .' some members of the congregation may say to themselves, 'Oh, dear. He's going to talk about divorce. How dull and depressing.'

But if instead you begin:

'When Margaret became engaged to George all her friends thought it was going to be an ideal match. Unfortunately, it didn't work out like that because . . .' you will probably carry every one of your hearers with you. However uninterested they may be in divorce *as a social problem,* they will all be interested in George and Margaret! And as they listen to the story of the break-up of this particular marriage they will begin to realize something of what is at stake in the institution of marriage as such.

But the story of George and Margaret will do more than crystallize a social and moral problem. Just because it is a moral problem, it will demand a verdict. You may ask your hearers for their verdict,[1] but even if you don't, most of them will find themselves taking sides, and forming their own

[1] As in the sermon on Barnabas, p. 62

judgements on where George was wrong and what Margaret ought to have done.

A well-told story can get more quickly and directly to a man's real self than any amount of argument. Indeed, the antiquity of the fable is itself evidence that our ancient forefathers recognized as clearly as we do that men's actions are motivated less by reason than by desire and imagination. The story gets below the purely rational level and appeals to those deeper springs of desire and impulse that are the real roots of character. Think, for instance, of the familiar incident of David and Nathan. David had done a particularly beastly and deplorable thing. He had seduced another man's wife, and to cover his guilt, had arranged that the woman's husband should be conveniently killed in battle. Nathan's task was to make David see how grievously he had sinned in the sight of God and man. But he didn't go and start 'telling him where he got off' as we might say. If he had, David would have been full of excuses and self-defence. Instead, the prophet told the king about a wealthy man who had seized a poor man's pet lamb, and at once David was bursting with indignation. 'What a perfectly rotten thing to do. The man that hath done this thing shall surely die.' 'Yes.' said Nathan, 'that man is yourself.' There was no answer to that. David saw the truth about himself *because he had first been made to see it in terms of somebody else.* Then he was judged, not by his accuser, but by his own conscience.

That is the psychology of the parable. As used by our Lord, the parable was often very far from being 'an earthly story with a heavenly meaning'. Some of his parables are not strictly stories at all. They are just simple everday illustrations and their meaning is often very earthly and homely. But they always express a truth that men don't easily recognize because they are themselves involved in it, in such a way as to enable them to see it objectively, and then if they have the honesty to do so, to apply it to themselves. When the Pharisees accused our Lord of lowering the standard of religion and respectability by consorting with publicans and sinners, he didn't say, 'Well, they're just as valuable to God as you are, and a great deal more responsive'. Such a reply would merely have alienated them still further. Instead, he appealed to their better judgement with illustrations of the principle at issue, the force of which they could hardly fail to recognize. 'What man who has a hundred sheep, if he lose one of them doesn't go out and seek it? Or what woman who misses a piece of silver from her necklace doesn't make a great to-do until it is found?' The answer is obvious. So is the implication: 'Well then, mustn't the same be true of God and his erring and wandering people?' The point about this kind of illustration, whether it is briefly presented as an analogy, like the lost sheep and the lost coin, or in a more fully dramatized version as a parable, is that it demands an answer, and an answer that must itself by a moral judgement – 'Is that true or isn't it? What do *you* think?'

Stories can be used not only to illustrate a truth, to appeal to conscience, or to convict of error, but also to arouse desire and kindle the affections. This last, possibly more than anything else, is the preacher's over-riding purpose. We shall never convince men simply by argument that Christian discipleship is more satisfying than the pursuit of money or power or pleasure, but the story of Matthew or Zaccæus or St Francis or Albert Schweitzer may arouse the beginnings of the desire to seek the pearl of great price. Argument may be needed to establish the truth. But persuasion, infection, and suggestion must be brought to bear if men are to desire it. Christian discipleship does not begin until the 'This is' of God's truth has become the 'I want' of the seeker. For this reason I am myself convinced that when we are faced, as we sometimes are on national or civic or similar occasions, with a congregation containing a proportion of people who make no Christian profession, we should rely much less on exhortation and argument, and make much more use of our Lord's method of speaking to them in parables.

4   THE ARRANGEMENT OF IDEAS

I have often been astonished at the number of preachers who wander aimlessly from one idea to another in apparent disregard of the fact that their hearers are expected to follow their train of thought! I have known a preacher get himself into such a confusion of ideas that the only possible way by which he could extricate himself was 'And so we see . . .', which we certainly did not!

Many who are much more disciplined and keep strictly to their theme appear to lack a sense of logical or pyschological progression. Here is an example:

The subject of the sermon is 'our need of God.' The preacher, very properly, begins where his hearers are. He reminds them of the common experience of finding that our achievements invariably fall short of our desires and expectations. We reach one goal or achieve one ambition and then look round for further fields to conquer. We gain one possession and the advertisers see to it that we're soon turning our eyes to a bigger and better model. Indeed the whole business of advertising is to make us dissatisfied. At a deeper level are those rare moments when a poem, a piece of music, a sunset, an encounter with a loved one, brings a glimpse of truth or beauty that stirs us to the depths of our being. We say 'Yes, this is the real meaning of life.' Like Shakespeare's Cleopatra we all have immortal longings. But they always elude our grasp.

The preacher then goes on to argue that this universal experience of dissatisfaction, these glimpses of the unattainable, of a vision never realised, is basically an unconscious and unrecognised hunger for God. He may quote Studdert Kennedy, 'I must have God. This life's too dull for aught besides.' And at some point he will (inevitably!) quote St Augustine, 'Thou hast made us for thyself, and our hearts are restless until they find rest in thee.'

It then occurs to the preacher that he ought to provide a specific illustration of the process which he has hitherto described in general terms. So he says, 'Take young George for instance. Like most youngsters of his age his great ambition on leaving school and starting work was to have a motor bike. He pays the deposit, signs the contract and that splendid "250 c.c. Yamaha" is his. He's now one of the fraternity. He is free to go places and see things hitherto beyond his range. But two years later he suspects that he is falling in love with Susan, and Susan doesn't like riding pillion. She doesn't think it safe. So the beloved motor bike has to give way to a second-hand Mini. At first George regrets the change. You *ride* a bike. You *drive* a car. But soon the advantages of increased safety, comfort and weather protection become evident. But so do the limitations of the Mini. He finds himself enviously eyeing the larger car with better acceleration and more sophisticated gadgetry. Well,' says the preacher, 'so you could go through the story of George's life as a car owner, and trace his progress from one car to the next, not simply because wear and tear make replacement necessary but because no sooner does he reach one level of satisfaction then another and more desirable make or model appears on the horizon' – and so on.

John Smith (at the end of the third row) has been listening to the story of George with rapt attention. It's in large measure his own story. He notes that the vicar himself must have been a motor cyclist to appreciate the difference between *riding* a bike and *driving* a car, and he begins to think about his own present car. 'The battery will need replacing soon. So will the two front tyres. Why not trade it in before incurring such expense? But in exchange for what?' He considers two new models recently come on to the market. One is a bit beyond his financial reach, but the other? He does some simple mental arithmetic, from which day dream the clatter of a hymn book dropped by a child on to the floor, suddenly recalls him to the fact that he is in church, supposedly listening to the sermon!

John Smith illustrates two hazards of which the preacher must be aware and for which he must try to make provision.

The first is this. Quite apart from the extent and duration of the mental side-track on which John Smith (and others?) was sent off by reference to the subject of motor cars, the preacher had wrongly plotted his course. He was leading his hearers in the wrong direction. What he should have been doing, and doubtless intended to do, was to lead his hearers from the familiar world of everyday things and experiences to the less familiar terrain of God and the things of God. What he actually did was to lead them in the wrong direction – from God to motor cars.

Of course in most sermons there are bound to be constant and a reciprocal movements from God to the world and from everyday experience to God. But these are or should be subordinate to the *main movement of the sermon.* It should start where people are and lead them to where the preacher wants them to be – nearer God. The main direction of the sermon should be God-ward. Having reached that glimpse of God's truth which the preacher is striving to disclose it is no reversal of direction to apply it to everyday life. So when planning the several stages of your sermon it is important to see that they are in the right order and lead step by step in the right direction.

5   KEEPING THE THREAD

The second hazard for which the preacher must try to make allowance is this. Everyone who has ever been to a church service or listened to a sermon will be familiar with this experience of having one's attention diverted from the matter in hand to a line of private reflection. There is hardly any subject you can mention or illustration you can use, hardly a verb or noun that you can utter that does not present a possible mental side-track to some member of the congregation. You cite the most commonplace experience, that of receiving a letter from a friend, and Jane (the churchwarden's wife) immediately thinks 'Letter. Oh, dear, I faithfully promised Elizabeth that I would let her know Margaret's new address in Manchester, and now she is gone and I forgot to ask her for it. I wonder how she is settling in Manchester; so very different from Norwich. I wonder if she is on the phone yet? Perhaps . . . Oh dear, what was it the vicar was saying?'

When Jane returns to your sermon, does she recognise the road along which you have been leading her? A bit further on – but the same road – the same line of thought? Or does she find herself in an altogether different scene and wonders how on earth you moved from the point at which she left you to the point where you seem to be now?

Some preachers have an unhappy knack of appearing to break their sequence of thought even when the sequence has been carefully thought out, because they have paid insufficient attention to the importance of 'links.' By this word I mean the phrases or sentences connecting one stage of the sermon with the next; the most critical of all being the passage from the introduction to the presentation. Take, for example, the sermon on St Barnabas (p. 62) and replace the first sentence of the presentation ('A very good illustration of this . . .') by: 'Tonight is the first Evensong of St Barnabas, and you may remember that he once had a quarrel with St Paul. It's about this that I want you to think, because it provides an excellent illustration of what I was saying a moment ago . . .'. It is immediately apparent that the substitution has created a break in the sequence of thought by the sudden interpolation of a new idea – 'Tonight is the first Evensong of St Barnabas'. The thread has been broken, and it will take the less percipient listener several seconds to realize that the break was more apparent than real. 'What's St Barnabas got to do with differences of temperament and having a common aim?' he will say to himself. 'Oh, I see. He's going to use him as an illustration'.

I remember hearing a sermon on prayer. The preacher was explaining that prayer is not simply talking to God, but also being quiet and listening; spending time in our Lord's company. Then he said, 'Bethany is a small village about two miles from Jerusalem. There was a house there where Jesus often used to go. It was the home of his friends Martha and Mary and Lazarus . . .' And he proceeded to relate the familiar incident of Martha and Mary.

Now *I* knew what was coming as soon as I heard the word 'Bethany'. But for the majority of the congregation there was not the slightest connection between what the preacher had been saying about prayer and the fact that Bethany is two miles from Jerusalem. The preacher's use of the illustration was good and it came at the right point of his exposition. There was nothing wrong with the arrangement of his ideas. Each step followed naturally from what had gone before. But at this point 'Bethany is a small village two miles from Jerusalem' – he *appeared* to be going off at a tangent. Of course, the congregation would soon realise that the deviation was more apparent than real. But why break the thread? All the preacher needed to have said was, 'There's an excellent illustration of this truth in the familiar story of Martha and Mary', or simply, 'Do you remember the story of Martha and Mary?'

It would be a counsel of perfection to say that the best way of keeping your hearer's attention is never to lose it. But it is unwise to make unnecessary demands on his powers of concentration by appearing to jump from one thought to another quite different thought. Where the presentation demands the introduction of a new line of thought, or if you are presenting two or three pictures not in sequence but for comparison, this should be made clear in the way they are introduced. For example: 'I want you to think of three entirely different reasons people give for not going to church, and see if you can discover what it is that they have in common. The first is. . . . The second is. . . . etc. etc.' It is important to keep the thread of the discourse clear and running smoothly from point to point.

6   THE USE OF 'I'

In the early days of my ministry the use of the first person singular in sermons was discouraged. Many considered it bad form and strenuously avoided it. I could see no reason for this self-denying ordinance, and in contexts where it seemed natural to use it I did so and still do. Today we seem to have gone to the other extreme. We live in an age which cultivates the ego and the subjective at the expense of traditional wisdom and experience. We see this on all sides, in art and music and religion, even to the extent of sheer unreason. The artist whose work bears no discernible relation to the external world replies to any such criticism by saying 'But that's how *I* see it'. The radical theologian who denies the reality of the Incarnation or the Resurrection appears in no way disconcerted by the fact that he is setting himself in opposition to the age-long tradition and authority of the Church, including very many men of vastly greater intellectual stature than himself. One recognises, of course, that the contemporary retreat into subjectivism is the individual's only defence against the pressures of a collectivist society in which he seems to count for little or nothing. But pursued, as it often is, in defiance of reason and corporate experience it can only lead to isolation and death. If I say, 'I find the music of Bach boring', I may truly be expressing my own feelings, but I am also revealing my appalling musical ignorance. We have reached a point in our intellectual and cultural chaos where it is essential to discover the true balance between the limitations and prejudices of the individual and the authority of corporate experience. In no sphere is this more vitally important than in that of Christian belief and morals. The old adage, 'I accept on authority and verify in experience', has been replaced by, 'My experience is the only authority I recognise'. The important question is not whether I can bring myself to believe in God, but whether God exists, and if I steadily ignore what those who are best qualified to know have to tell me about God, I am likely to remain in doubt.

The preacher who is constantly thrusting his own doubts and difficulties upon his congregation is abusing his authority and betraying his commission. The sermon is not the place to work out one's own conflicts. Its purpose is to proclaim the Gospel.

On the other hand, preaching, as has already been said, is an essentially personal matter. The preacher is not a lecturer handing out knowledge in which he may not be personally interested; he is a man addressing his fellow men in the name of the Lord. And while he does not speak on his own authority, he must speak from his own conviction and experience. However much he may use such phrases as 'the Church teaches' or 'Christians have always believed', his preaching would have no power if there were any thought in his mind, let alone any suggestion in his manner, that he was not convinced of it himself. It is true that he does not speak simply by virtue of his conviction. He can only preach in the congregation if he holds some recognized office as licensed reader or ordained minister. But this fact in no way diminishes the necessity of speaking 'as man to man'. There is a further fact that is true of most preachers, viz. that he is also a pastor speaking to his flock, a father instructing and guiding his family. Any diminishing of the personal element that may result from stressing the truth that a priest preaches by virtue of his office and not by virtue of his gifts, is more than made up by the fact that he also preaches as a pastor. St Paul uses the first personal pronoun a very great deal, but never more than when he is acutely aware of his apostolic and pastoral responsibility. To some degree, therefore, preaching presupposes an I-You relationship.

But the preacher is not only a pastor and teacher, he is also a fellow pilgrim walking the same way of life as those to whom he speaks. It would appear presumptuous, and it would also be dishonest, if he did not frequently identify himself with their struggles and temptations and failures. If therefore, 'I' occurs often in his sermons, 'we' should be no less frequent. My impression is that many preachers today use too much 'I' and too little 'we'. A friend assures me that his young incumbent is constantly quoting 'my Mum'!

AFTER THE SERMON

I have been unable to trace the origin of the custom of ending the sermon with the ascription, but I am quite sure that a critical examination of this time-honoured practice is long overdue. In particular, there are two considerations that would suggest a revision of our accepted ideas about what ought to happen at the end of a sermon.

First: To talk about religion is not the same as religion. Religion is relationship with God. For this relationship no amount of religious knowledge is a substitute, nor does its possession give any guarantee of personal relationship with God. Second: When we are preaching or teaching we are speaking of God in the third person – 'he', 'him'. But religion is something that takes place in the second person – 'you', 'thee', 'thou'. We can talk about God (in the third person) until we drop with exhaustion, but nothing has happened by way of religion until some soul has said in his heart, 'Lord, look upon me. Lord, I come to thee'.

Surely the logical and psychological place for this transition from the third person to the second is *immediately* after the sermon. Indeed, the better the sermon, the more necessary it is to give the hearer a brief period of time in which to turn the truth he has gained from it into terms of his own approach or committal to God. Suddenly to say, 'And now to God the Father, God the Son . . ., etc. Hymn number forty-eight', is to cut short the mental and spiritual process with which the congregation ought to have been kept busy during the sermon, at the very moment when it ought to reach its climax in personal approach to God. A sermon (very many sermons, at any rate) ought to make people want to pray. If the preacher gives them no opportunity to do so, he has to some extent defeated his own purpose.

It may be argued that a sermon preached in the course of a service is already within the context of relationship with God. But the service itself (be it Mattins, Evensong, or the Eucharist) is a blend or alternation of affirmations made about God (in the third person) with acts of praise and prayer and penitence (in the second person). Broadly speaking, canticles, hymns, and prayers express the response appropriate to the statements made about God's saving acts in the Lessons, Epistle, or Gospel. The purpose of the sermon is to select one particular aspect of the Gospel for special consideration; as if the preacher were to preface his sermon by saying: 'Everything we have done and said and sung, indeed our very presence in church, is based on the great fact of our redemption, and of all that God has done to restore us to himself through Christ. Now let us think of one particular aspect of this saving truth'. The aim of the sermon is to particularize, to focus attention upon some selected aspect of the total gospel.

We have already noted that the preacher's purpose is to secure a verdict. But that verdict is addressed not to himself but to God. So let the preacher get out of the way and give his congregation the opportunity to make their response direct to God. The sermon should therefore be followed not by the ascription or some traditional formula which for many congregations has become no more than a conventional signal to shuffle to their feet, but by a short time of recollection and prayer: a quiet 'Let us pray' and (when the congregation has knelt or remained quietly sitting) a brief bidding, a short silence, and then a carefully chosen prayer or collect. Incidentally, if a collect really does 'collect' the thoughts and prayers that have been prompted (and, if it doesn't, it shouldn't be used), its words will light up with new and deeper meaning to many people. Sometimes a short scripture reading may be the most appropriate vehicle for guiding the message of the sermon into the final act of prayer or praise.

At this point many readers will want to say, 'This may well apply to sermons preached at Mattins or Evensong. But nowadays the majority of sermons are preached at the Eucharist'.

This raises an issue of liturgical usage in which the compilers of the ASB seem to me to have displayed a remarkable lack of pastoral sensitivity, viz. the juxtaposition of the creed and sermon in the Eucharist.

On what conceivable grounds did they change the 1662 order?[1]

Was it because the creed is the summing-up of the Scripture readings and the ministry of the Word? An equal case could be made for the creed as the summary of the Scripture readings. Yet how much better, as in the 1662 order, for the preacher at the end of the sermon to be able to say 'Let us pray. . . .' followed by a period of silence introduced by the briefest possible bidding, and then after the silence to move naturally into 'Let us pray for the Church and the world. . . .' Placing the creed after the sermon instead of before it is in my view a thoughtless piece of pedantry, and in practice it is clumsy. The congregation stands for the Gospel, sits for the sermon, stands up again for the creed and then kneels for the prayer for the Church. How much more natural to stand for the Gospel and the creed, sit for the sermon, then kneel for prayer.

What are we to do about this? One way is to discuss the question with the congregation. If they take the point (I should be very surprised if they did not) then it can be agreed that the sermon shall follow the creed. If however the incumbent and/or the congregation feel that duty demands following the prescribed order of Rites A or B, then have a period of silence after the sermon while the congregation is still sitting.

Be that as it may, and be the sermon ever so carefully prepared and compellingly delivered, its value may well be lost unless it is followed by a short period of silence – a silence in which the preacher gets out of the way, and the souls of his hearers are left face to face with God alone.

---

1 There is no argument to be derived from liturgical tradition. The place of the creed has varied at different times and in different parts of Christendom. The earliest usage (4th–6th cents.) was to recite it after the offertory. Charlemagne introduced it to Gaul in the 8th century where it came immediately after the Gospel. At Rome the creed was not recited in the Eucharist until the 11th century. Cf. Dom Gregory Dix, *The Shape of the Liturgy* pp. 485 to 488.

Chapter 7

Preparation and Delivery

We have already studied the processes of thought by which a sermon is shaped, and there is no need to repeat them, except to offer one or two practical suggestions about their week by week application.

The incumbent who sees his preaching as a long-term responsibility[1] rather than a week by week duty will be in large measure delivered from the element of anxiety in the inescapable question, 'What shall I preach about on Sunday?' He will of course have to make such a decision but he will not be making it, so to speak from cold, or in a vacuum. He will have an overall picture of the ground he wants to cover in a particular period, and many of his sermons will be grouped in threes or fours to deal with subject matter that could not be comprehended in one address. Nevertheless the question of 'What?' and 'How?' will still have to be answered every week and he will be wise to reach his decision *early* in the week. For myself I am never very happy unless by Monday evening or Tuesday morning I am quite clear about the 'What?' of the following Sunday's sermon.

[1] See Chapter 9.

Having reached this decision I then let it simmer, turning over possible ways of the 'How?' at odd moments. Usually I make a list of all the revelant reflections, incidents, illustrations, etc., that come to mind as described on pp. 58–60 in relation to St Barnabas. This process of considering various possibilities and finally selecting the material and method most suitable to one's purpose is the first, and in many ways most exacting, stage. If it is not done on paper it must certainly be done in the mind. My own experience has been that it was only after years of scribbling down and crossing out on paper that I found myself able to do much of it in my head without recourse to pen and ink. This stage of the process is rather like packing for a holiday. You lay out on the bed all the things you think it would be nice to have with you. Then comes the moment of decision. This item is too big for your case. That is too heavy to carry. Those would be pleasant to have with you, but you reject them as superfluous to likely need. In the end you leave more on the bed than you pack in your case![1] In other words, you probably find that you have enough material for one or more other sermons! In which case you have to ask yourself: Is this theme of sufficient importance to justify a further two sermons. or is this one sermon adequate to fulfil my purpose?

Much here depends on the length of the preacher's experience and the width of his reading. In one's early years it is not always easy to find enough relevant material for one sermon, let alone two or three! But continued reading, praying, familiarity with the Scriptures and pastoral experience steadily increase the 'stock' on which one can draw. Indeed most of us would agree that our experience in this field illustrates the truth of two familiar sayings:

1 'To him that hath shall be given'.
The better stocked and co-ordinated your mind in a particular field the more rapidly you acquire fresh knowledge.

---

[1] I owe this illustration to Canon M. E. Dahl whom I heard use it in a lecture many years ago.

2 'The best way to learn a subject is to teach it'.
The need to communicate knowledge to others makes you
think about it more critically than you otherwise might, and
drives you to go on thinking, sorting out the essentials from
the non-essentials, co-ordinating and ordering your material
until you are quite clear about what it is that you want to
communicate.

In the process of selecting the material you need you have
probably found that you have gone some way to answering
the question of *how* you are to present it. For example, in
choosing St Francis as your best illustration you are thereby
deciding that part at least of your presentation will be in
narrative form. You then have to ask yourself: Is the story of
St Francis sufficient by itself, or do I need a modern parallel
or contrast to put beside it? Or will the story of St Francis fail
to make the point unless I lead up to it by a certain amount of
preliminary discussion of the point at issue? It may well be
that you cannot settle this question until you are clear about
how the truth with which you are concerned is to be applied
to the lives of the congregation. The various stages of the
sermon are now beginning to take a logical shape. There
remains the question of how best to introduce your subject in
such a way as to engage your hearers' attention and keep it.

When by this process you begin to see the sermon as a *whole*
it should then be set out in precis form in its three stages:

INTRODUCTION

PRESENTATION

APPLICATION

Before writing it in full or making a fair copy of its outline
for use in church, the preacher should submit his work to a
searching examination on the lines of the following questions:

1. Is the purpose of the sermon sufficiently clear?
2. Has it a good SHAPE? Are the steps or stages in the
   right order? Will it engage the hearers' minds from
   beginning and lead them step by step to *seeing* the truth
   at issue? i.e. Is there a *disclosure* as distinct from mere

assertion? What about the ending? Is it clear, definite, and related to contemporary Christian living?

3. Has the sermon an element of *kerygma* or theological content?
4. Is there sufficient appeal to desire and imagination? i.e. Is it likely to move anyone?
5. Is there any point which requires an illustration to make it clear?

OUGHT THE SERMON TO BE WRITTEN?

When any necessary changes have been made we are faced with the question; Ought the sermon to be written out in full (if this has not already been done) or can it be preached from the précis with possibly additional expansions?

There may be some few men having such a command of language and a gift of speech that so long as they are clear about what they want to say, can say it well, and for whom the business of writing would be tediously superfluous. But such men are few, and for most of us it would be a danger to assume that we are of their number. Most of us during the first few years of our ministry should accept the discipline of writing the sermon in full.

The skeleton sermon, though now complete as a process of thought, has yet to be expressed in words, and until a man has acquired that facility in expressing his thoughts with the clarity and force that is normally only acquired with practice, he will be well advised to do his practice in the privacy of his study before he ventures into the pulpit. Moreover, it's not simply a question of finding words, but of finding the right words, and arranging them in the most expressive form. The young preacher who gives up writing too early in his ministry runs a great risk of producing loose constructions and a limited vocabulary, constantly dropping back into the same stock phrases. The process of writing will give time for choice of the right words, and allow of attention not only to phraseology but also to rhythm and balance. Having written the sermon, it is a wise plan to read it aloud; the sound of it will indicate where an arrangement of syllables is dissonant (if the preacher has an ear for such things), where sentences need shortening and words altering and where such other detailed polishing and pruning needs to be done. It is by careful attention to these matters that the young cleric will increase his command of language, and acquire the ability to express himself clearly without having first written down what he wants to say. Every hour or so spent in his first years will pay rich dividends later.

The pulpit, however, is a very different place from the study. The thoughts and prayers that have made the sermon in the study have in the pulpit to be transformed into an act of living communication to people. In the study it is the thought that is foremost; in the pulpit it is the people who become all-important. That is why the sermon, however carefully written, should never simply be read. It should first be learned, and then be *preached*. The learning is not nearly so formidable a task as might be supposed by those who have never done it. When a sermon has first been thought out, then written out, and afterwards read aloud, the preacher should already almost know it. Two or three subsequent readings should then suffice to give him a crystal-clear picture of what he wants to say, and a fairly large command of the language in which he proposes to say it. When he gets into the pulpit he must speak *to his people* of what is in his mind and heart. The fact that his manuscript is in front of him will almost certainly lend him confidence, but an occasional glance should be all that is necessary to keep him going. There are some preachers who develop such skill in reading their sermons that the congregation is unaware that the sermon is being read, but the danger of being too dependent on your manuscript is that you are not sufficiently free for that giving of yourself to your people, which is the essence of all effective preaching. It may well be that, having written his sermon and thoroughly digested it, the preacher will be able to deliver it with the aid of only brief notes or headings.

Where, as in some parishes, it is customary to deliver the sermon from the chancel step or in front of the altar with no lectern, notes may be an embarrassment to the preacher, and he will have so to have mastered his sermon as to be able to deliver it without them. To do this effectively requires not less work than the use of full notes or a manuscript, but more. He will need to have the whole sermon clearly in his mind, not because he has learned the words by heart, but because he sees in his mind the sermon as a whole and knows how he is going to express it.

There is, however, one part of the sermon which even the most experienced extempore preacher will be well advised to write in full and get clearly into his mind – the ending. We have all listened to the preacher who goes on talking after he has come to the end, with the result that he becomes counter-productive.

The application of the sermon is the point to which it is directed. It is the preacher's reason for preaching it. Let this therefore be unmistakably clear, and as briefly and cogently expressed as possible. Also, as I said earlier, it makes for a sense of artistic unity and strengthens the impact of the sermon as a whole if there can be some brief reference to the experience or question or text with which the sermon began. It is not always possible to do this. Where it is possible it is always worth doing.

So whether he uses his manuscript or not, the young preacher, unless he is exceptionally gifted, will be well advised not to be in too great a hurry to spare himself the labour of writing his addresses in full. I have myself been preaching for nearly half a century, and often have had to speak or lecture for fifty or sixty minutes using only very brief notes or none at all. But I still write in full a fair proportion of my sermons, and I find that the discipline of doing so stands me in good stead for those occasions when such writing is impossible. It is illustrations and methods of presentation that I have sweated over in the study that have come to my aid in mission preaching, answering questions after lectures, and similar circumstances in which the use of notes was not possible.

THE USE OF LANGUAGE

The need for 'starting where people are' has an obvious relevance to the question of language. Many of the criticisms made about sermons are provoked not by their content but by the language in which they are presented. When people say of a preacher, 'He's above our heads', they may mean either that his thought is too abstract or that his language is too obscure. Either of these is a fault, but the latter is the more serious. If your meaning is plain, your hearers may be able to follow you even though you take them into unfamiliar realms of thought. But if what you say does not make clear what you mean you have lost all hope of taking them anywhere. Every preacher should strive, like St Paul, to 'use great plainness of speech'. But plainness in this context does not mean vulgarity or poverty; it means clarity. Say what you mean. Don't hint at it, or imply it. Say it, and say it plainly.

How far this much-to-be-desired directness of speech should be idiomatic, even at times slangy, is a question that must remain, to some extent at least, a question of taste and, in any case, must depend on circumstances. Some subjects are capable of an informal method of presentation, idiomatic language, and a relatively light touch. Others, for example, the Passion of our Lord, are not. Nor would one expect to address a congregation most of whom read only the picture papers in quite the same language as a congregation which almost entirely reads *The Times*. In general, however, it is true to say that, while nothing is to be gained by going out of one's way to be crude and spicy, a good deal is to be lost by studiously avoiding current idioms and phrases on the ground that they are undignified. They probably are undignified, but just because they are common coinage they carry a significance and a pungency that no circumlocutions can achieve. Moreover, slang phrases are often symptomatic of people's basic attitudes to life. What an unconscious articulation of the bewilderment, the disillusionment, and the consequent irresponsibility of this generation is the current trilogy of phrases, 'I haven't a clue', 'You've had it', and 'I couldn't care less'. The preacher who never uses such phrases will leave an impression of remoteness from his people. The preacher whose sermons are too frequently interlarded with them will seem too nearly identified with the attitudes they connote to be a reliable guide to a realm of life where such sentiments would never be heard! Let us then learn to say what we want in the simplest and most direct way, using the speech of everyday rather than the language of the theo-logical text-book: not 'This principle is capable of further extension' but simply, 'Another thing . . .'; not 'the Pauline Epistles' but 'St Paul's letters'. Spurgeon gave good advice to his students when he told them never to use a sixpenny word when a threepeny one would do.

It is, however, important to recognize that the informal and conversational type of sermon does not require any less careful preparation than its more dignified brother. It may indeed demand a more deliberate effort on the preacher's part to express himself in homely language and current categories of thought. There is a deal of difference between the preacher whose direct and simple language is the result of careful thought and skilful preparation and the preacher who chats amicably and informally because he has only the vaguest idea of what he proposes to say. In preaching, as in most other crafts, there is an art that conceals art.[1]

Few temptations that beset the preacher are so insidious as that of saving ourselves the trouble of thought and explanation by the use of jargon and clichés. We find ourselves dropping into such phrases as 'Christ's victory over death', 'the offering of our daily lives', 'the guidance of the Holy Spirit', without ever having explained to our people what any one of them means. It is, of course, impossible to teach the Christian faith without making use of such words as Incarnation, Sin, Grace, Salvation, etc., and it would be

---

[1] John Austin Baker's sermons in *The Whole Family of God* (Mowbray 1981) are an inspiration not only in their content but in their use of direct yet powerfully suggestive and evocative language.

tedious in the extreme to have to define them on every
occasion. Such words are Christian technical terms and their
meaning should be known by every Christian. But it is a wise
plan often to refer to them by an explanatory phrase, 'God's
coming in Christ', 'Man's rejection of God's authority', etc.
Similarly, we shall be wise not to talk overmuch of 'our sins'
or 'Christian graces', but to be specific and speak instead of
'pride, jealousy of others, selfishness at home' or 'love, joy,
peace, gentleness, and self-control'.

We need to remember, too, that words are used not only to
convey our meaning, but also to suggest attitudes, emotions,
and overtones (or undertones) of approval or disapproval.
Political speeches and newspaper articles provide daily
illustration of the attempt to influence people's thinking not
so much by the facts reported as by the manner of their
presentation. The speech that in one paper is described as 'A
staunch defence of Church principles' in another becomes
'The same die-hard obstinacy'. We cannot ourselves dispense
with or avoid such suggestive and emotional use of language.
Indeed, no small part of a speaker's skill is his choice of the
right words. But we shall be wise occasionally to remember
that oratory can be a very dangerous art, and discipline
ourselves to use words with a sense of responsibility. In a
world in which language is prostituted to many base ends,
and is often used unscrupulously by politicians, journalists,
and advertisers, we must beware of the temptation to pay the
world back in its own coin by being equally unscrupulous
ourselves. Our language should be as cogent, as colourful,
and as compelling as we can make it, but it should be chosen
with due regard both to our own and to our hearer's integrity.
We shall not attempt to jockey him along with mere words,
and we shall be honest in argument. If we are stating an
objector's case, we shall be careful to state it fairly and meet it
squarely. St Paul's advice to Timothy needs repeating to
every generation of preachers: 'Give diligence to present
thyself approved unto God, a workman that needeth not to
be ashamed, handling aright the word of truth.'[1]

[1] 2 Tim. 2.15

Nothing that I have said about the use of language should be taken to justify the practice of 'talking down' to our people. It is better to be slightly above rather than below the level of their intelligence. The same is true in the sphere of moral and devotional response. We should not hesitate to make clear that we expect the highest possible response from them. It is no compliment to them to expect little, and they will quickly come to distrust the preacher who asks less of them than they are capable of giving. Rightly so, for the demand of the Gospel is uncompromising. While, therefore, it is usually a wise plan not to take too much knowledge of Christian doctrine for granted, it is essential always to assume an earnest intention to make the highest possible response to our Lord.

DELIVERY

Having written at such length about the principles and technique of sermon-making, it is humiliating to have to admit (as honesty compels me to do) that the delivery of a sermon is almost as important as its content. Like most generalizations, such a statement is subject to a measure of qualification. A good presence coupled with an interesting and well-modulated voice can hold the attention of an audience even if the speaker is talking piffle; so much so that his hearers probably don't realize that it is piffle! Contrariwise, a man who is obviously a master of his subject will be listened to with unflagging concentration by an audience that wants what he has to give, even though his speech and manner may be monotonous to a degree. But while neither of these extreme sets of circumstances is normally found in the parish church, there are some men whose local reputation as good preachers rests almost entirely on the vigour and colour of their delivery, and there are others the excellence of whose material is unappreciated by their congregations because their speech is flat and their manner heavy. It is little short of a tragedy that a man who has laboured to prepare a good, instructive, and inspiring sermon should fail to get it over when he comes to preach it, because he has never realized the important of taking trouble over delivery. Though the clerical monotone and the special voice have mercifully almost entirely disappeared from Anglican pulpits, there are still far too many of us who have not yet learned to speak naturally when we are preaching. By 'naturally' I do not mean speaking *exactly* as one speaks in ordinary conversation. Public speaking demands a slight exaggeration of the variation of the tones and inflections of normal speech simply because of the greater distance between the speaker and the hearer. For the same reason the preacher will have to speak more slowly in the pulpit than in every day conversation, and the larger his church the slower his pace will have to be. But his variations of pace and of light and shade will be of the same kind as those of ordinary speech, not some special pulpit blend. There is, of course, a place for the occasional period of unashamed declamation, and for the touch of genuine drama when the subject or occasion demands it. Moreover, it should be apparent in our manner that we are preaching because we have something to say, that we are gladly under divine constraint to say. But eagerness and passion are far removed from ranting. Few things are more wearisome than listening to a preacher who declaims all the time, or who dramatizes the most commonplace remark.

It is perhaps worth noting that, as Canon Douglas Cleverley Ford used often to point out in the College of Preachers residential courses, there are three distinct uses of the voice in Church.

1. Liturgical

The reading or recitation of liturgical prayers is by definition impersonal. They are not the reader's words but those of the liturgy. He should not therefore attempt to impose his own interpretation upon them or express his personality through them. Imagine the havoc that could be wrought in the prayer of St Chrysostom (BCP) by a reader who was intent on giving dramatic prominence to 'who dost *promise*' or 'when *two or three* are gathered in *thy name* thou *wilt* grant their requests'! This does not mean that such prayers should be recited in a flat deadpan voice. It simply means that they should be said intelligently and prayerfully, using no more than three tones of the voice and making use only of such phrasing and emphasis as the sense of the words demands.

2. Reading

There was a time when, in reaction to an earlier cult of declaiming the Scriptures, clergy were taught that the same liturgical impersonal voice should be used for reading the lessons. The result was to kill them stone dead!

Today, aided by the use of modern translations we read more intelligently. Yet though most of us read reasonably well, there are very few who in my experience read really well, and with anything like sufficient vitality. Better even to 'preach' the Scriptures than to read them as if they were instructions on the bottle. There is no need to declaim. Nevertheless it is our privilege and duty to articulate the meaning inherent in the printed word. Narrative should be read as narrative, with some light and shade about it. The words of the speaker should obviously be 'in inverted commas'. Poetry should be read as poetry; drama as drama. Phrases that are antitheses should appear so. It is my firm conviction that the arguments of St Paul's Epistles can be made as clear by an intelligent reading aloud from the Authorized Version as they can be for the silent reader by the use of a good modern translation. There's no need to be theatrical in order to convey a sense of drama. To learn to read aloud and to read well is to form the basis of a good delivery in preaching. I entirely subscribe to Canon Cleverley Ford's dictum: 'If you can't hold people's attention at the lectern, you are not likely to do so in the pulpit'.

3. Preaching

In preaching 'it's all yours'. You are commending the truth as *you* see it, it is *your* message. Hence the relevance of what has been said above about being 'natural' in your inflections, even though the size of the building may make it necessary to speak much more slowly.

A word of caution here about amplifying systems. The great advantage of the microphone is that it enables the preacher to retain the natural tones and inflections of the voice which would otherwise render him inaudible in a large building. But it does not – repeat not – mean that he can therefore speak at the speed of normal conversation. The presence of amplifiers allows for much more colour in the voice but it does not alter the *pace* of delivery imposed by the building. Many preachers seem unaware of this, with the result that their words are little more than a jumble of only partly intelligible sound.

Here let me put in a word of practical advice. Before beginning your sermon, give the congregation ample time to get settled in their seats, and even then don't be in a hurry to start. Within reasonable limits the longer they wait for you to begin the greater their degree of expectancy and attention! When you do begin, begin slowly, so as to ensure so far as you can, that you retain their attention and direct their thoughts along the line you want them to follow.

The first requirement is that the preacher should speak clearly and be easily audible; the second is that he should speak naturally; and the third is that his voice and manner should convey his own interest in his subject, and his conviction of its truth. If the preacher doesn't *sound* interested in what he is saying, he has no grounds for complaint if his congregation isn't interested either. The preacher who has had any experience of sound broadcasting will know something of the discipline imposed by the fact that he cannot be seen by his audience. Whatever he doesn't get over purely by the use of his voice, doesn't get over at all. Since the advent of the tape recorder there is little excuse for any preacher not submitting himself from time to time to the same discipline. It is a very salutory experience to hear yourself as other people hear you. A preacher can learn more by spending a couple of hours with a tape recorder than from any amount of written advice about proper inflections and variations of pace.

These admonitions, however, do not cover the whole of preaching. Their aim is merely to ensure that the preacher has learned (or will take trouble to learn) properly to use his vocal instrument. But it is no more than an instrument. A clean, well-modulated and interesting voice will not of itself convey inspiration or passion if these things are not in the preacher. But the man whose passion and inspiration are inhibited by a colourless manner of speaking is like a musician forced to play on a piano that is out of tune and has half its notes missing. Learning properly to use your voice is like learning the principles of preaching.[1] Neither of these arts can by itself create anything. Each is simply a medium of expression, and its purpose is to ensure that such love of God as fills your heart and such truth of God as illuminates your mind can freely communicate themselves to your people. As with the principles of preaching, so with the control and use of the voice – once they have been mastered by conscious practice, they become unconscious, and it is not until they do become unconscious that they are truly instrumental. Once you have learned properly to use your voice you can be conversational, meditative, prophetic, or passionate, as occasion demands of the spirit of God prompts.

READING

It may seem a serious omission that so far I have said nothing about reading. That any priest who, year in and year out, is to preserve an alert and well-informed mind *must* keep up his reading is so obvious as almost to be taken for granted. No one can be constantly giving out unless he is also steadily

---

[1] A preacher who finds himself frequently suffering from a strained or sore throat is probably producing his voice wrongly, and should consult a speech therapist.

taking in. Nevertheless there are two things that perhaps should be said, however briefly:

1. The preacher who becomes dry and devoid of ideas is in the majority of cases the man who has neglected his reading. The simplest way to 'keep up one's reading' is never to let it drop. Always have a spiritual or theological book on the go. The more hard pressed you are the more necessary it is, and the easier it is to make use of the odd half hour between engagements. You just carry on with the book, bit by bit, until you have finished it. Then start another.

Putting it baldly, in this didactic manner, I seem to have represented reading simply as a duty, a necessary part of the preacher's job. Well, it *is* a duty. Those who are ordained priests in the Anglican church make a solemn promise to be diligent in prayer, in reading the Scriptures and pursuing such studies as will deepen faith. But to regard such study simply as a duty is completely to miss the point. It is a constant challenge and a never-ending delight. How enormously fortunate we are in being able to regard it as part of our work! Let me explain what I mean. Every craftsman, every worker in the field of art or science or medicine or engineering is always seeking more skill, more knowledge, fresh insight. Part of the fascination of all such work is the awareness that the more one knows the more there is to know. Similarly every thoughtful man wants to make sense of life, and every thoughtful Christian wants to make sense of his faith, not to have 'all the answers' (he never will) but to have a sense of congruity between his Christian belief and his experience of life; to see the world and the life of man through Christian eyes, to have a Christian picture or philosophy of life. The Christian layman will want to do this. The Christian preacher *must* do it. Like St Paul he must have *a* gospel, his own grasp of *the* Gospel. What a privilege to be able to pursue this never ending search as part of one's work. For myself, I have never been attracted to jigsaw puzzles. Yet in a wider sense I spend my life doing one, constantly discovering in reading and personal encounter new pieces that

I can or cannot fit into the whole picture. The former are a delight. The latter are a challenge. The fact that reading spiritual and theological books suggests valuable subjects and material for sermons is almost incidental. I am grateful for them and often make a note of them for future reference. Nevertheless the main and overriding purpose of reading and thinking is to deepen one's hold on the faith and to widen one's vision of the Gospel in relation to the varieties of human experience and the constantly changing climate of contemporary opinions and assumptions. It is an inexhaustible fascination. How often I find myself saying of some new insight, 'Good heavens. Why have I never realised this before?' Or of some new challenge, 'I've got to come to terms with this.' The bishop who said, 'When I go into a man's study I cast an eye over his bookshelves, to find out when he died', was a bit too sweeping. It's not necessarily the newest books that are the most fruitful. But he had a point. There is a sense in which it is true to say that when a man stops reading and thinking, then he does die. A man needs this for the sake of his own soul and his own intellectual integrity. The pastor needs it more urgently than most because he has so often to help other people in their doubts and difficulties. It is of the *modus operandi* of the media to publicize the sensational and the controversial. The doubts of some prominent ecclesiastic or the sceptical speculations of a scholar to whose views, be they never so aberrant, prestige is given by the title 'Professor' or 'Doctor', these things are *news*. The solid faith and weighty scholarship of those in the main stream of Christian belief are not. When the man-in-the-pew finds himself confronted on TV by some way-out cleric who blandly denies the existence of God or the historical reliability of the Gospels, to whom is he to turn if not to his priest or his pastor? What more need be said about the pastor's duty and privilege to remain a life-long student of the Word of God and of the foundations on which it rests?

2. It often happens, however, that we want to 'read up' the subject about which we intend to preach, or to check our

facts. In this case my advice is: Never begin by 'reading up'. Always begin by jotting down your own thoughts, your own grasp of the point or truth at issue. You then have something to which your reading may be related, and you may want to alter or amend your original idea in light of further knowledge. The danger of *ad hoc* reading before you have attempted to sort the subject out in your own mind is that you may end up in muddle and confusion. So always clarify your own thoughts first.

It would be idle to pretend that the fact of having to produce at least one sermon a week is not an ever-present factor which influences one's reading, thinking, praying and everyday experience. It does. But not, it is to be hoped, at the conscious level. It would be dreadful and disastrous consciously to approach one's reading and daily experience with the question: 'What can I say about this?' or 'How can I make a sermon out of it?' Nevertheless, awareness of the need to be able to give an account of one's faith does unconsciously lend an additional urgency to the impulse to make Christian sense of life. Every thoughtful Christian, by the very fact of being a Christian, will be seeking consciously or unconsciously to relate the joys and tragedies of life as he experiences them in his own life as a man, a husband, a father, a worker, or encounters them in the lives of others in personal contact or via the media, to his Christian understanding of the nature and destiny of man, and of God's mysterious work of creation and redemption. Being a preacher will simply make this process rather more conscious not least because of his responsibility to help others to interpret life Christianly. My own habit, described on page 74 of seeking concrete illustrations of truths encountered in abstract or theoretical terms is not consciously related to my preaching. I developed it simply as a way of seeking to deepen my own understanding. Yet it was doubtless the necessity of having to preach and teach that lent added urgency to my desire to clarify my understanding.

What I am trying to say is that though the final notes for,

or the manuscript of, one's sermons may be written in the study, *preaching is not a product of the study but of one's whole living and thinking and praying.* This is no less true of the lay preacher than it is for the parish priest. The latter will have more direct pastoral contact with the people to whom he preaches. But in the office or on the shop floor the layman has experience and relationships not normally available to the priest. So the layman who is a preacher is by that very fact also a pastor.

For the preacher who is thus a true shepherd and who is constantly feeding his own mind and soul by reading, prayer and pastoral contact, there is no danger of growing stale or 'running out of ideas'. He will, of course, have his occasional periods of dryness and weariness. We all do. But he will never feel that he has nothing more to give. Most of us who have had ten, twenty, thirty or forty years experience of preaching know that we have hardly begun either to master the art or to explore the inexhaustible riches of the Gospel.

WHAT IF YOU HAVE MORE THAN ONE SERMON A WEEK?

It may be objected that in much of the foregoing I have assumed that the preacher has only to produce one new sermon a week. What about the man who has to produce two or more? Evensong may be dwindling in numbers but it is not dead, and the people who come have every right to expect a sermon and that mainly from the vicar, even if occasionally he makes use of a reader.

One answer is simply to say that the vicar has to do twice the amount of sermon preparation! I do not regard this answer as realistic. For two reasons:

1. I do not believe that most of us are capable of producing more than one original and well thought out sermon per week. In most parishes there are far too many things that have to be done.

2. This is not simply a question of the time available,

measured in terms of hours at our disposal, but of what I can only call 'mental time'. For myself, I have always found that when (as far too often!) I have had to produce two or sometimes three addresses in the week, it is one of them which really occupies my mind and fires my imagination. The others recede into a subordinate position, and I can only give my mind to them when the first has been completed. I suspect that this may be true for many of us.

Much depends on the circumstances of the parish. If the evening congregation is entirely different from the morning one, then the morning's sermon may well be adapted for use in the evening. If not, then it may well be that a series of sermons produced some years earlier may be brought up to date and adapted for the evening congregation. I see no objection to this. To those who say, 'I can never re-preach an old sermon' I reply, 'If that's how you feel about it, it would be fatal to attempt to do so. But why does it seem to you 'old' or 'stale'? Because it is 'dated' or because you no longer see that particular truth in the same way? Then why not try to express the same truth as you now see it? At least that old sermon gives you something to work on, and that's easier than having to start from scratch.'

My own experience leads me to put a further point. I have often preached what is virtually the same sermon to different congregations.[1] Yet it's never the *same* sermon, not only because one automatically adapts it to the particular congregation, but because of the part which the congregation plays in the total work of preaching. Preaching is essentially a relationship between preacher and congregation. It is a giving and receiving. The receiving is no less important than the giving. Those who have given much the same course of lectures to a variety of audiences will know how different from its predecessors each delivery proves to be, not only in

---

[1] Not, it is important to add, because I have not had time or energy to produce something else, but because it was the message I was eager to deliver. Unhappy is the man who does not *want* to preach his sermon!

terms of receiving but equally of giving. A point taken quickly by one audience needs to be expanded and illustrated for another. And the questions often afterwards asked by members of the audience provide the lecturer with criteria for revising his lecture: Ought I to anticipate this question, or is it better to leave it to be dealt with as a separate question likely to be asked again?

The point I am seeking to make is that if the preacher has to provide two sermons a week, one of which is the *main* sermon and the other subordinate, I see no reason why he should hesitate to use material from earlier sermons preached to a different congregation. The one qualification is that to whatever extent it needs to be recast it must result in a sermon he *wants* to preach.

If the circumstances of the parish or the priorities of the preacher's mind do not allow of any such distinction between *main* and *subordinate,* then my advice is this. Make your decision of the 'What' of *both* sermons at the very beginning of the week, so that both can simmer in the mind, but complete the 'How' of the first before starting on the second.

Chapter 8

Preaching and the Old Testament

When I was a curate in Norfolk, in the early thirties, I used periodically to be invited to preach at a girls' boarding school. The service was Evensong but the lessons bore no relation to the lectionary. They were chosen by the headmistress, and I soon came to realise that the selections from the Old Testament which she considered suitable for her pupils were drawn almost entirely from Isaiah or the Wisdom books – 'Ho everyone that thirsteth come to the waters' – 'Remember thy Creator in the days of thy youth' – and so on; passages which, in her view at least, could be torn from their historical context and yet still appear relevant and edifying to young ladies of the twentieth century.

At the time I sympathised with her because I was myself often embarrassed by having to read some of the more bloodthirsty bits of the OT to the congregation in the parish church. Looking back I now realise that neither she nor I had begun to come to terms with the OT. Nor, incidentally, had either of us understood the purpose of the lessons in the Office of Evensong.

Nevertheless, still has my sympathy. Because although I now realise that we were both wrong in our attitude to the Old Testament, it is one that is still prevalent among modern

Christians. The problem for many modern churchpeople is the fact that the OT is 'in the Bible'. The fact that both the Old and the New Testaments form the Church's canonical Scriptures and are both regarded as 'the Word of God' seems to suggest that the ritual regulations of the Book of Leviticus or the record of tribal battles in Samuel and Kings are of equal importance to the Gospel of St Mark or the Epistles of St Paul – which is manifest nonsense. But how do you get round it? In what relation does the OT stand to the NT that allows both to be regarded as sacred Scripture? And what place has it in Christian worship and preaching?

This is the basic question. But it is a question that some clergy and teachers never really face. There are several ways of evading it. One is to do what the headmistress did – ignore the bits that you don't like and select what seems appropriate. Another is to use characters and incidents from the OT as pegs on which to hang Christian or moral teaching; to quote the child Samuel as an illustration of listening to God; to use Saul to point out the dangers of jealousy, and Haggai's exhortation to complete the restoration of the Temple as an example of putting the worship of God before all other considerations – and so on and so on.

But, it may be asked, why should we bother to do all this spiritualising of the OT when we can get all we need from the NT? In any case, if you are only using the OT to find *Christian* meanings, you *are* discarding it – unconsciously. So why not face the fact: leave the OT on one side and stick to the NT?

The answer is, of course, that no conscientious priest or pastor can adopt such a policy. It would be both a denial of the truth and also a repudiation of his ordination vows.[1] Yet what is he to do? The Gospels and Epistles and Acts are

---

[1] A comparison of the Ordinal in the BCP with that in the ASB will reveal that while the promise to base his preaching and teaching on the Scriptures is more explicit in the former, the vesting of the newly ordained priest's authority on the Bible is no less implicit.

clearly his source-book for the life, teaching, death and resurrection of our Lord and the faith of the early Church. He can base his sermons on them and his hearers take it for granted that he should. They see no such direct line connecting the OT to the present day. Hence it is with the preacher's relation to and treatment of the OT with which we shall be concerned in this chapter.

Let us begin with the fact that whether our congregations realise it or not the Christian faith and the Bible (the whole Bible, not just those parts of it which may be considered relevant or useful) are inseparable. To question this is to question the nature of the Christian faith and nearly two thousand years of Christian conviction and experience. You do not need to be a fundamentalist in order earnestly to desire to see and strive for the recovery of a much greater use and veneration of the Bible than is to be found among many Christians today. We have everything in our favour – new translations and all the resources of historical and scholastic research. The 'criticism' of the Bible that leads us astray is not the work of the scholars but the largely unconscious presumption that we have nothing to learn from the men of the pre-scientific (and therefore unenlightened!) past, even about their experience of God who, presumably has not changed his nature and purpose to keep step with modern progress.

Yet even if we were not inhibited by our modern assumptions from that due humility which for Christians has been regarded as the proper approach to the Bible, there is a further problem – our contemporary ignorance *of* the Bible.

It is not so long ago that some knowledge of the Bible was regarded as a constituent element of English culture and education. Biblical allusions and phrases formed part of our everyday speech and reading. Indeed many simple folk knew much more about Abraham, Isaac and Jacob, Saul, David and Solomon, than about the history of their own country. Why? Because of the Scripture readings to which they listened at Morning and Evening Prayer every Sunday.

Before I became a theological student I cannot recall ever seriously *reading* the Bible. But I was thoroughly familiar with a great deal of it, at least up to the period of Exile, because I had heard it read Sunday after Sunday in church. The modern churchman who goes only to the Parish Communion gains no such familiarity with the OT. The laudable attempt on the part of the compilers of the new liturgies to introduce an OT lection fails on two grounds. The first is that (in my view at least) *three* readings are more than most people can take in. The second is that because the OT reading must be kept short, the compilers have little option but to follow the principle of the headmistress and select short passages mainly from the prophets which even when divorced from their historical context have a thematic relation to the NT readings and some immediate relevance to modern Christians.

So the preacher is faced with an inescapable question. We cannot present authentic Christian faith *apart* from the Bible. How can we help our people to a sufficient familiarity *with* the Bible that will enable them to learn something of what God has to say to us *in* the Bible?

I do not believe that the answer lies simply in trying to give a biblical flavour to our preaching, being studious to begin every sermon with a text. Neither shall we achieve this aim by basing every sermon on some scriptural incident or confining it to a demonstrably biblical topic. Moreover, whatever we do, we are like the headmistress and the compilers of any lectionary, faced with the necessity of selection. There is not time to read or preach the whole Bible and there are large sections of it that would not make very profitable reading even if we could. What is needed both by the preacher and the congregation is a *principle* of selection, a guide or map that will enable us to find our way through its rich diversity. We need (to use the analogy yet again!) to be sufficiently familiar with the wood as a whole in order to know which of the trees bear fruit for our nourishment. This involves a deliberate and sustained effort to rescue the Bible as a whole from the fog of ignorance and unreality with which it is surrounded in the minds of many of our people, and to plant it firmly and clearly in its proper place as providing not only the liturgical material of our common worship, but the very *raison d'être* of our membership of Christ and his Church. When this has been done, there may emerge a new kind of expository and exegetical sermon. But until then, most of us will have to spend at least as much of our time preaching *about* the Bible as we spend preaching *from* it. Not that these two approaches are mutually exclusive. A sermon can be both from the Bible and also about it. All that I am concerned to emphasise at this point is that there are certain things our people need to know *about* the Bible before they can begin rightly to receive *from* it.

But where does one begin with so vast a subject? How much and what kind of background knowledge do people need before they can receive from the Bible with understanding and spiritual profit?

There are at least three questions that we must try to answer – and go on answering:

1. In what sense is the Bible authoritative?
2. What is the relation of its various parts to the whole (and of the whole to the parts), especially of the New Testament to the Old?
3. What is our relation as Christians today with this book which was written so long ago?

All this is very much easier to describe than it is to carry out in practice. For example, the first item in the above summary involves tackling the problem of a 'chosen people', so alien to our contemporary climate of thought. The modern man feels not only that it was 'odd of God to choose the Jews' but that God had no business to discriminate, that all nations should have been started off fair and square in the best democratic tradition. We can only deal with this difficulty by considering the relevant facts.

The question 'How do you know that God exists?' looks like a question about God. In fact it is a question about the validity of human knowledge. Our knowledge of God comes to us in exactly the same way as our knowledge of everything else. All our knowledge is derived from two processes: experience – all that we can see and hear and read and touch and taste, and reason – the faculty of interpreting the things of sense experience. Our knowledge of God derives from the same two sources but with one vital difference. God is not susceptible of human examination. He is beyond the range of our senses. We can know nothing of God unless he takes the initiative in making contact with us and making himself known to us. It is the unique claim of the Christian faith that God has done precisely this, even to the extent of himself becoming a man, speaking our language, living life, sharing our suffering and death and that he did this not only in order that we might know what kind of God he is, but also in such a way as to overcome our habitual resistance to acknowledging his claim on our love and obedience.

But for God to come to earth as a man meant that he had to come at some definite time to some particular place. Did it matter when or where? Of course, it mattered essentially. No good purpose would have been served by his coming to a people who believed that God was the-man-in-the-moon! They would have been able to see no possible connection between a God up there in the sky and a man walking on two feet. It was necessary that God should come to a people possessed of some capacity for recognising him for what he was. But where were such people to be found? They did not exist. They had to be chosen and trained. How? God could not trust to some kind of spiritual broadcasting in the hope that some sensitive soul here or another there would see a gleam or hear an echo of the divine truth. What guarantee was there that the gleam would not fade and the echo die away with the death of the aforesaid sensitive soul? As a matter of fact God did make considerable use of particular individuals, *but only after he had created a living community to which the prophet could speak with some confidence that his message would find permanent lodgement.*

Here was a task needing a continuing community that could and would pass on the fruits of one generation's experience to the next. Again, since the truth of God that men needed to know could only be learned in life, it had to be made part of life; it had to be *practical* not simply *theoretical*; it had to be intimately related to daily life and religious practice, to moral obligation and personal responsibility. Such is the slowness with which we learn from experience that this task of preparation took twelve hundred years. This is the purpose that Israel was chosen to fulfil – to be the people prepared for the coming of God-in-man.

This at least is what Christians believe. Can we sustain such an astonishing and to many modern people unfashionable claim? Consider the no less astonishing fact that several centuries before the great thinkers of Greece came to the conclusion that there could be only one God, the much less intellectually gifted people of Israel claimed that he had made a covenant with them. On purely evidential grounds the weight and extent of this testimony is so impressive as to create a strong presumption of its truth. If one or two outstanding individuals, a Moses, an Isaiah or a Jeremiah, claimed that they had encountered God and enjoyed a personal relationship with him, such an assertion might be explained away as the exhibition of abnormal psychology or strange hallucination. But the witness of the Old Testament extends over a thousand years and has a unanimity that is quite remarkable. Eight hundred years separate Moses from Jeremiah, but the God to whom each bears witness is the same God – a God whom they had come to know not because they were looking for him, but because he had made himself known to them.

On the natural level, the life of ancient Israel had much in common with their contemporary neighbours in the Fertile Crescent. Their legal tradition bears many resemblances to that of their Babylon conquerors. Their sacrificial system had elements in common with the Canaanite people whose land they made their own. Yet Israel's faith was unique. In a world peopled with gods, some benign, some malign, the God of Israel stood alone and supreme. He was a God of action. He had rescued them from slavery in Egypt and entered into a covenant with them. Moreover he was a holy and righteous God. He cared for the poor, the fatherless and the widow, and demanded a similar moral response from his people. But – most significant of all – he was a God who *speaks* to men and seeks a personal relationship with men, a God not only to be worshipped and obeyed but also to be loved.

From whence did the men of Israel derive the picture of such a God so utterly different from the gods of the ancient world? Certainly not from any religious or theological genius that they themselves possessed. They were a people of a particularly pragmatic and untheological turn of mind. Indeed the prophets would have said that it the people of Israel had any genius for religion, it was a genius for constantly falling away from it! It is simply impossible to account for the phenomenon of Israel except that they were indeed chosen by God to receive a special revelation of himself. Have we modern men, whose moral standards and conduct fall far below that of the Ten Commandments, nothing to learn from them? Does the state of the world today provide the slightest evidence that the advent of science and technology has taught us anything more about the essential meaning and purpose of human life than they possessed? It is not that Israel is important because of the Bible or the OT. It is that the OT is important because of Israel. They were the chosen people, chosen not *instead* of the other nations, but *for the sake of* the other nations. That is why, when God entered human life and history as a man, he came not to Rome or Gaul or Greece but to Palestine. Everything our Lord said and did took for granted what Israel alone among the nations knew. When he spoke of God, the Father and Creator, he did not mean what the Greeks or the Romans meant by the word 'God' – he meant the God of Abraham, Isaac and Jacob, who had showed his ways unto Moses and his works unto the children of Israel. When he spoke of 'faith and 'righteousness' he meant what the prophets of Israel meant by those terms. To no other nation in the world would our Lord have made sense. That is why we cannot begin to understand the New Testament apart from the Old Testament. Hence the Bible is like a two-act play. The second act depends on the first, but the first by itself is incomplete, as the OT by itself is incomplete. But we cannot understand the New Testament without the Old. Our sole authority as preachers lies in God's action of self-revelation to the people of Israel culminating in Christ and verified in the experience of the Church.

In Chapter 9 I shall argue that we cannot possibly hope to discharge the whole of our preaching responsibility in one brief sermon – or even two longer ones – per week, but that some provision must be made for supplementary basic teaching. Let me here plead the cause of using such a course to give a birdseye view of the Bible with special attention to the Old Testament. It can be done in six or seven sessions divided up like this:

1. THE AUTHORITY OF THE BIBLE. Variety of views of the 'Word of God'. How is God to communicate to man? (as pp. 113–115) History–Christ–Church. Our title deeds.

2. THE COVENANT PEOPLE. The foundation of Israel's belief – deliverance from slavery in Egypt (the possible volcanic explanation of the plagues). The divine 'coincidence' of Moses. The covenant on Mt Sinai.

3. THE PROMISED LAND. The invasion (?) of Palestine. Judges v. Joshua. The theological problem: 'Can Jahweh grow corn?' The social and economic pressures to acknowledge the Baals.

4. THE KINGDOM(S). The Philistine threat and the need for central leadership. Saul, David, Solomon and the rebellion which divided Israel from Judah.

5. THE PROBLEMS OF SURVIVAL IN A WORLD OF POWER POLITICS. The Assyrian invasion and deportation of the Northern Kingdom. Elijah, Elisha and Baal worship. Social conditions and the protests of Amos and Hosea.

The Babylonian threat to the continuing existence of the Southern Kingdom. The work of Jeremiah and Isaiah. Josiah and 'the Book of the Law'.

6. THE EXILE – THE END OF THE STORY? The Jews in Babylon and the work of collecting and editing of the historical records and the teaching of the prophets. The beginnings of 'Scripture'. Ezekiel, II Isaiah and the Return. The work of Ezra and Nehemiah. Haggai and Zechariah.

7. THE OLD TESTAMENT IN THE NEW. Brief summary of the period between the Testaments. The revolt of the Maccabees. The social and political scene into which our Lord was born. His implicit and explicit fulfilment of the OT – 'not to destroy but to fulfil'. The New Covenant.

Laid out in this way the course might appear more suited to students preparing for a Scripture examination than for hard pressed lay folk. But there is no need to make an academic study of it. It's a story! The most moving and dramatic story in the world. The human ingredients of this story are those that we encounter every day and in every newspaper and novel that we read, men and women with their hopes and fears, joys and sorrows, their sins and virtues, their kindly and their cruel deeds. What distinguishes the Bible is that it sees this human drama, so to speak, from God's point of view and in relation to God's will and purpose for men here and hereafter. As Studdert Kennedy once said, the Bible makes better reading than the News-of-the-World if only because it tells of another world. What a gift to a preacher! Let him recount it simply and with full appreciation of its drama, not simply as history but as the interplay of God's initiative and man's response. Especially is it necessary to make clear as the story proceeds the message and work of the great prophets and their place, not only in their immediate historical situation, but in God's unfolding purpose for Israel. Not every member of every congregation will give up six or seven evenings to receive such enlightenment. It is my experience however that a surprising number are not only grateful for such help but ask for more.

Incidentally, when commending such a course to a group of clergy I have often been asked, 'Do you use visual aids? Slides and pictures of the ancient world and its people?' My answer is always an emphatic 'No'. To do so would merely throw into prominence the difference between their circumstances of life and ours. My purpose is to emphasise their essential likeness to us, sharing the same basic humanity with its hopes and fears, loves and hates, joys and sufferings.

The only visual aid (apart from a map) I use – and I regard it as essential – is a *time-chart* showing (vertically) the line of Israel's history through the centuries, numbered from c. 1220 (the Exodus) to our Lord's birth BC/AD. The line breaks into two at the division of the Kingdom, the short leg representing the brief existence of the Northern Kingdom, the story being continued through the long leg with a clean break for the Exile. At the side of this long chart the centuries are marked 1000, 900, 800 etc. and on the other side are printed in their appropriate places the great names – Saul, David, Solomon, Amos, Hosea, I Isaiah, Jeremiah, Ezekiel, etc. It is also a help to have the periods of Assyrian, Babylonian, Greek and Roman domination distinguished by backgroung colour washes.[1]

It may be objected that such a course, however valuable, can only be done once and is therefore only one item in an ongoing ministry of several years. By no means. It may well be repeated every three or four years, not only for the sake of new people coming into the congregation but because it need not and should not be a mere repetition. The preacher is himself presumably growing in his knowledge and understanding of the Bible. Of course the main facts and events – the Exodus – the Settlement – the Exile – the Return – will remain the fixed framework. Yet each time the story is retold it can be done with a different emphasis. One

---

[1] A similar chart may be found in *The Lion Handbook of the Bible.*

presentation may be directed to showing how God was gradually preparing his people for his coming in Christ. Another may be directed to illustrating how God is continually 'getting through' to men, despite their sins and stupidities.

At some point also we must deal with the truths and insights which the men of Israel preserved in parable and story, viz. the truth of God as Creator and man as his rebellious creature (the stories of Adam and Eve, the Tower of Babel and Noah's Ark) which form the prologue to the Bible, together with the great themes enshrined in the stories of Job, Jonah and Ruth. The special nature of and the message contained in the apocalyptic books, Daniel and Revelation, might well feature either in a systematic course or in separate sermons.[1]

My point is that, whether the preacher embarks on such a systematic course or not, its main outline must be clear in his own mind and emerge in his preaching. It is by no means an insuperable task by constant reference to the historical background to give our people a reasonably clear picture of the main events of Israel's history. When dealing with any Old Testament theme of character it is always necessary to paint in the historical background. Amos was not addressing his impassioned plea for social justice to us, but to the exploiters of the poor and the 'get rich quick' men of the kingdom of Israel after the Syrian war. It was against the threat of the growing might of Babylon to the little kingdom of Judah that Isaiah said 'Trust in God, not in treaties of mutual defence with Egypt'. The relevance of this past history is what God has to say to men in such circumstances. What do we know of power politics, the barbarity and destruction of war, the plight of refugees, or famine, of corruption in the high places and of flagrant social injustice that the people of Israel did not experience in their chequered history? The weapons of war, the scenery, the clothes, the

---

[1] A useful presentation of these themes will be found in William Neil's *Can we trust the Old Testament?* (Mowbray 1979)

dialogue – these all change, but the characters, their hopes and fears and passions and ambitions, remain. Love and hate, hope and fear, birth and death, marriage and parenthood, achievement and failure, selfishness and self-sacrifice – these are the stuff of human life, and they remain basically the same for all men in all ages. What does it matter that one set of men travel on camels and another in cars and aeroplanes? What does it matter that one set of men reckon their wealth in flocks and herds and another in stocks and shares? Our concern is not with their trappings but with the essentials of life, man's destiny and God's purpose.

In presenting the Bible, therefore, we must use every bit of skill at our command to show that its people are real people, fellow-sharers not only in God's mighty act of redemption but also in our hopes and fears, trials and temptations, joys and sorrows.

The first need is to make clear the close similarities that exist between the situations in which the people in the Old and New Testaments found themselves, and the circumstances that surround us today. There need be no special pleading or rhetorical artifice about this. The parallels do exist. Just because human nature changes so little in the course of the centuries, the situations in which people become involved in their personal and social relationships are repeated again and again.

The second task of the preacher is to drive home the force of these parallels by presenting them in *modern* language and idiom. The use of modern translations is undoubtedly an enormous help in making the Bible 'come alive'[1]. Nevertheless the preacher in re-telling an incident can use a much greater freedom of contemporary idiom and analogy than would be appropriate to the translators. Did the men of Israel never use the equivalent of our slang? Let us suppose that we are telling

[1] For the private reader I should unhesitatingly commend the Jerusalem Bible in preference to the others, because of the invaluable headings it provides for each section and subject.

the story of Nehemiah. We have explained his background as a second generation exile and his employment in court service; we have told of how he had spent a sleepless night agonising over the dreadful plight of Jerusalem, news of which had just reached him. Then he comes in to serve the king's breakfast.

'Hallo', says the king. 'What's the matter with you, this morning? A bit liverish, what?'

'No, sir, thank you.'

'Well, what is it? Tummy?'

'No, sir, thank you.'

'Dash it, man, there's obviously something wrong with you. You look as if you hadn't slept a wink all night. Are you worrying about something?'

'Well, yes, sir. The fact is, I've just had some bad news. The city of my fathers . . . etc., etc.'

My point is that, although we must be faithful to the historical situations to which the Word of God was addressed to the prophets, we can and should feel free to use every legitimate device to help our hearers really 'get the feel' of these situations. For instance, I have no hesitation in picturing the young and aristocratic Isaiah moving about in 'the fashionable drawing-rooms in Jerusalem' and the glamorous young women eyeing him archly and saying, 'Dear Isaiah, how too, too naughty of you to say such things about us'. The pedant might say, 'But they didn't have drawing-rooms!' Of course they didn't *call* them that, but how else is one to describe the equivalent which they certainly had?

Similarly, in dealing with the NT background, to describe Corinth as the Liverpool, or Ephesus as the Edinburgh of the ancient world is to by-pass the circumstantial and architectural differences, because they are irrelevant, and direct attention to the human likeness, the polyglot population with its dock workers and ship owners, its trading houses and its brothels of the one, and the treasured traditions and civic pride of the other.

In this Chapter I have been concerned with the OT because of the difficulties it presents to many preachers. I am not for a moment questioning the fact that by far the larger part of our preaching and teaching must inevitably be based on the NT. The authority of the Bible for Christians is vested in Christ. Indeed, my insistence that we must preach *about* the Bible as well as *from* it, applies no less to the NT than to the OT. In particular modern Christians need to be helped to realise the importance of the Pauline Epistles. So many of the reconstructions of Christian faith being offered as more relevant to the needs and presuppositions of modern man are based on a highly selective treatment of the synoptic Gospels, and almost entirely ignore the Epistles. Thus is created the impression that the Gospels are the foundation Christian documents, and that the doctrines contained in St Paul's Epistles – relating to being baptised into Christ's death, the new creation and membership of the Body of Christ – are a later and less trustworthy addition, interpreting the events recorded in the Gospels. We know and our people ought to know that the Gospels were written for those who had already received *the Gospel* of life in the risen Christ through membership of his body the Church. Here is a common misunderstanding we must seek to correct in our preaching.

A very interesting and instructing course of sermons can be based on the Acts, beginning with the question 'Given the events recorded in the Gospels and culminating in the Resurrection – what then? What should we *expect* to happen afterwards?' Then look at what actually did happen, with special reference to the work of the Holy Spirit in the young church, and putting the writing of St Paul's letters into their proper place in his missionary activities. It is also important to explode the commonly held notion that the Gospels were written so long after the events they describe as to render them unreliable[1].

It is, however, needful to remind ourselves that, fascinating

---

[1] I strongly recommend Bishop J. A. T. Robinson's *Can we trust the New Testament?* (Mowbray 1977) which deals succinctly and authoritatively with this question.

and rewarding as the task of making the Bible come alive may be, its purpose is not simply that of teaching history, even Church history. While the Church and her faith can never be separated from their roots in the historical redemption which God wrought within the stream of human history, and of which the Bible is the sole record, the relevance of that redemption to ourselves lies in the here and now. The fact that we now recognize the Bible to be a record of God's saving acts, rather than a compendium of divine oracles, must not be taken to mean that there is no longer any sense in which it contains a 'Thus saith the Lord'. For the history of Israel differed from that of ancient Assyria, Babylon, Greece, and Rome precisely in the fact that its people were made to see the crises of their national life in terms of the purpose and judgements of God. It is not simply that the long training of Israel was a necessary preparation for the Incarnation, and that it is therefore impossible to understand the New Testament apart from the Old. It is not simply that the Bible is thus our own history as members of the Covenant-People. It is that in the whole process of this saving-history culminating in Christ and issuing in his Church there is to be discerned a divine pattern which is itself a revelation of God's nature and purpose. The preacher must therefore be concerned with the Bible not only as the history of our redemption – the story of God and the People of God redeemed in Christ – but also with the Bible as the revelation of God's purpose in and God's judgements upon our present life. To use the Bible only as the record of what God once did, and to stop short of asking what we may learn therefrom about what God would have us do now would be a most serious dereliction of the Christian preacher's duty. Indeed, it is this attempt to apply to our present circumstances the truths which emerge from the divine pattern of the Bible history that constitutes the prophetic element in preaching, and distinguishes it from teaching *qua* teaching on the one hand, and from mere exhortation on the other. It is not a bibliolatry that we seek to inculcate, but the Bible view of life, the view that sees all human actions and events in the light of God's judgements and God's purpose. We do not want our people simply to stare at the lantern. We want them to be able to use it to illuminate their paths in life.

Chapter 9

Planned Preaching

There is one inescapable tension with which every Christian pastor has to live and which cannot be far from his mind in every sermon he preaches, viz. the tension between proclaiming and accepting the Christian faith on the grounds of history and reason, on the one hand, and personal commitment to Christ on the other. We have already argued (Chapter 3) that no man is a Christian simply because he has intellectually accepted the Christian claim. He must still enter into a relationship with Christ.

In Chapter 12 of his invaluable book, *The Foolishness of God,* the Bishop of Salisbury has shown how the historical circumstances in which the early Church came to birth made it necessary for the theological claims about Jesus to precede the moral recognition and acceptance that is the basis of Christian living. 'Instead of making conviction of truth dependant on commitment to the moral demand, the moral demand was presented as deriving from a prior conviction of the truth.'[1]

He then goes on to maintain that we still tend to persist in the same policy of erecting 'dogmatic hurdles at the entrance to the Church', whereas experience shows that belief in the Christian creed is more often a result than a pre-condition of membership.

[1] *The Foolishness of God.* J. Austin Baker, p. 320 (D. L. T. 1970)

There is a great deal of truth in this criticism. Yet it is difficult to see how the hazard to which the Bishop draws attention could be avoided. Indeed I believe there are two factors which render the danger less real today than it was a few years ago. One is the widening gulf between the Church and what it stands for on the one hand, and the aims and assumptions of secular society on the other, with the consequent discouragement from being identified with the Church. The other is the growing number of live and caring Christian congregations which are attracting a small but steady stream of hitherto unattached people.

Be that as it may, we are not thereby absolved from our duty to preach the Gospel and to provide our people with the intellectual and spiritual equipment needed to maintain their faith and nourish their life in Christ. It is for this reason that I make no apology for my repeated use of the terms 'instruction', 'doctrine' and 'foundations of faith'. I have yet to hear of any conference of laity that did not at some point ask for 'more teaching'.

The vicar[1] of a large town parish recently invited four members of his congregation to engage in a study of what the concept of 'shared ministry' meant in terms of the respective functions of vicar and laity. In due course the Group of Four, as they were called, produced a report stressing the need for a real sharing of ministry in relation to preparation for baptism, confirmation and marriage, and visiting, etc. The priorities they allotted to the vicar were *'study, preparation and teaching'* (italics mine). The more drastically the number of full-time stipendiary clergy is reduced, and the Church's pastoral work shared with the laity and voluntary assistants, the more necessary it will be for the declining number of professional priests to exercise a ministry that is – and is seen to be – primarily spiritual and theological. The extraordinary initial sales of the ASB, exceeding all anticipation, are evidence of a desire on the part of our lay folk to seize on any

[1] The Revd. Robin Brown, Vicar of St. Andrew's, Luton.

help that is made available to them. Indeed the danger of what Bishop Baker calls 'erecting dogmatic hurdles at the entrance of the Church' is no less real than the opposite danger into which many clergy fell not so long ago, viz. that of assuming that everybody knows what the Gospel is and on the basis of that assumption preaching sermons on love and faith and forgiveness with little mention of the saving truths of which these things are the fruits.

HAND-TO-MOUTH PREACHING

How is the preacher to set about the essentially pastoral task of enabling his people to know their faith and to live it? Let us begin with an analogy. Suppose you had little idea of the main development of English history through the ages, but were exposed to a weekly brief lecture on such varied topics as:

    The foreign policy of Elizabeth I;
    The social consequences of the Industrial Revolution;
    Was Richard III responsible for the murder of the Princes in the Tower?
    The Peasants' Revolt;
    Charles I King and Martyr?
    The murder of Thomas à Becket.

How much more enlightened would you be? You would doubtless pick up bits and pieces of the story, some of them very interesting, but you would still be lacking in a conspectus or picture of English history *as a whole* into which these episodes can be fitted and their significance appreciated.

Very many members of our congregations are in precisely this position in regard to their faith. Every Sunday they listen to sermons on entirely unrelated topics, a list of whose subjects would read rather like a table of contents in the average weekly periodical:

    Faith – Is it auto-suggestion?
    The story of blind Barimaeus;
    Can a modern man believe in God?

'Blessed are the poor' – a sermon on simplicity of life;
Do Christians believe in immortality?
Martha and Mary;
Science and religion;
What is the authority of the Bible today?
'Love not the world.'

There is little to be said for this kind of preaching. Very many congregations have grown accustomed to it, and some of them may mildly enjoy the element of surprise occasioned by the fact that they haven't the foggiest idea what the vicar is going to preach about until he starts. But is it not better that they should know, especially if they know that he is going to deal further with a subject in which they have already become deeply interested? The fact is that, with the possible exceptions of blind Bartimaeus and the Bethany sisters, none of the subjects listed above can be dealt with to anybody's satisfaction in one sermon. Most of them require a minimum of three, some of them at least six, sermons for adequate treatment. Further, the cleric who preaches in this snippety fashion can only say the most obvious things about his subject, and when (by the law of permutations and combinations) he finds himself back at the same subject again, he will almost inevitably tend merely to say the same things again.

The only way out of this vicious cycle of superficialities is to take as many sermons as are needed to deal with each subject satisfactorily. By so doing he will win from his congregation the response that comes from the knowledge that he is treating them seriously and taking pains to give them systematic instruction in their faith.

This is easy to say. It is by no means so easy to do. Later on we shall have to consider how to deal with the practical difficulties that have to be met if we are to have any hope of doing it. Meanwhile let us consider the psychological principles at issue.

THE WOOD AND THE TREES

We have already seen that the hearer's mind must be prepared to receive the truth that the preacher is setting out to present, by calling into consciousness some cognate knowledge or experience to which this new truth is to be linked. It follows as a corollary that this new truth must bear some relation to the relevant knowledge already possessed by the hearer. It is no use handing out information unless people already have some knowledge of the subject to which it can be attached. The growth of knowledge is like that of a tree, not like a pile of bricks. Unless there is some organized system of knowledge of any particular field of experience to which each fresh piece of information can be organically related, it will be regarded (consciously or unconsciously) as irrelevant, and will find no lodgement in the mind. What, for example, can the man in the pew make of a reading from Jeremiah (in the Old Testament lesson), if he has no knowledge of Israel's history, and therefore no idea of the circumstances in which Jeremiah lived and taught? What can a man make of a sermon on the Holy Spirit if he has not yet grasped the truth of the Incarnation? I suspect that much of our teaching fails in its purpose because many of the congregation are not in possession of a sufficient corpus of Christian doctrine to provide a foundation on which to build. The result is not an ever-growing edifice, but just a heap of bricks. Or, to change the metaphor, they do not realize the significance of the individual trees, because they've never seen the wood as a whole.

Suppose I were faced with a weekly catechumenate class of people desiring instruction in the Christian faith. The one thing I would not do would be to begin with God, creation, sin and so on, working steadily through the doctrines of Incarnation, Atonement, Church, and Sacraments. Why not? Surely such a method is logical, and each new step would build on a foundation that had been laid in previous weeks? Yes, but the class would not begin to see the point and purpose of the Gospel until we had arrived at least as far as the Atonement. Further, it is inevitable that many of the questions they would want to ask could only be answered in the light of truths not yet reached in the course. I should begin, therefore, with as brief and clear a statement as I could provide *of what the Christian religion as a whole is all about*: relationship with God, through Christ – a relationship for which man was created, but which has been broken by his repudiation of it, etc., etc. I should hammer away at this during the first two or three weeks until I was assured that my pupils had some idea of the essence and purpose of the Christian religion as a whole. Then – and not till then – would I begin to fill in the details. To change the metaphor again – get the skeleton first; let them see the shape of the body. Then clothe and adorn it.

GOSPEL SERMONS

What this principle means in practice, it seems to me, is that every so often we should preach a sermon which sets out the Gospel in miniature; an occasional pause in our Sunday by Sunday examination of particular trees in which we stand back and look at the wood as a whole.

It may be objected that you cannot possibly put the whole Gospel into one sermon. No, but you can encapsulate the heart of the Gospel in such a way as to make clear what the Christian faith essentially *is* as distinct from the common misunderstandings that are in circulation. The point to be stressed is that the Gospel is a declaration of divine redemption, not an exhortation to human moral effort. Each such sermon should stress the same basic truth in different contexts. The following half a dozen examples will indicate the kind of thing I have in mind. It should however be clearly understood that each is a synopsis, not a full outline.

SERMONS ON THE GOSPEL

1. It may seem superfluous to say that the Christian religion is primarily concerned with God. But listening to a great many discussions on 'the relevance of the Church' etc. etc., leaves one with the impression that it is concerned with almost everything *but* God!

   The question which the Gospel answers is not 'How can we live more comfortably and securely? How can we avoid war? How can the world be made safe for democracy?' but – 'How can sinful man be restored to the God who made him, and so regain the life and destiny for which he was created?'

   To imagine, as most people do, that Christ is simply a teacher or a good example is to make nonsense of the Gospel. If Christ is not, as Christians maintain, God-in-human-life why should we obey his teaching rather than that of Confucius or Karl Marx? And to think of our Lord primarily as a model for us to imitate is to be guilty of blasphemous presumption. To say this is not to deny that there is anything to be *learned* from the Incarnation. The first thing that we *learn* is that in Christ God has *acted* and that we are *involved*. 'The Son of God became the Son of Man in order that the sons of men might become the sons of God.'

   What the Gospel offers to men therefore is not an exhortation to moral effort but a *relationship with God*. It says not 'Try harder' or 'Be a better chap' but 'Accept Christ, and enter into the life of relationship.' *Then* our Lord's earthly life and teaching will become supremely relevant to them. But not before.

2. 'I'm just as good as those who go to church.' Maybe, but the Christian religion is not primarily concerned to make men *good*, but to restore them to their true relationship with God. Only then will they *want* to be 'good', that is, to do the things that God asks of them, not to justify themselves, but to please him.

   The great contrasts of the New Testament are not between good men and bad men, but between the Old Adam, and the New Man in Christ; between man fallen away from God and man restored to god.

3. How we all go for the latest 'news'! But it will be stale tomorrow. Nobody wants to read yesterday's newspaper.

The Church is the bearer to each generation of 'news' that never grows stale. The word *Gospel* means 'good news'. What of? Of God and his Kingdom. Of what he has done through Christ to open his Kingdom 'to all believers'. Of the new status made available to each generation in or through the Church, whereby we are enabled freely to approach God and to live as his children.

To those who accept this Gospel it is always 'new' because they are constantly discovering in it fresh depth and richness.

4. 'We're all children of God'. Are we? St John (1. 12) does not appear to think so. We are God's 'creatures' – yes. But we are not 'sons' until we accept our sonship in Christ. The parable of the prodigal son is a picture of man's age-long desire to get away from God, to run his own life, and be his own master. In this condition he is 'not worthy to be called thy son'; he cannot approach God as Father.

Christ took upon himself our human nature so that through him we could return to God as sons. (Compare 'May I introduce myself to you, Sir? I am a friend of your son'.) 'No man cometh unto the Father but by me.' Hence St John – 'To as many as received him, to them gave he the power to become sons of God. . . .'

5. 'What is a man to believe? The Churches all teach different things.'

Yes, there are differences. But if a man were to begin by getting his teeth into what *all* the Churches teach in common, he'd have quite a lot to be getting on with!

Though there are differences among Christians about *how* a man should respond to the Gospel (differences about such things as Church discipline, the place of the sacraments, the use and understanding of the Bible, etc.), all orthodox Christians are agreed about the essentials of the Gospel itself – that man was made to find his joy and delight and significance in the God who made him; that, instead, man has tried to find the meaning of his life in himself; that Christ came to make available a way of restoration to right relationship with God, etc., etc.

6. How many people spend a great deal of their lives wishing that things were different? 'If I had a car I wouldn't have to spend so much time waiting for buses', 'If I had a bit more money, I could go abroad for my holidays', etc., etc.

Many people put the Christian religion into the same category. They think that the burden of its appeal is – 'If only men would do right and be more unselfish, then we should have a better world'. Nothing could be farther from the truth. The Christian religion is not an IF religion, but an IS religion. It is concerned with things that ARE because God has acted to make them so.

The Bible is the record of what God has done to make possible the restoration of man to right relationships with himself . . . in the here and now, etc., etc.

Let no preacher assume that because he has done this kind of thing two or three times with the same congregation, it won't need doing again and again!

Another way of keeping the fundamental of religion in the forefront of people's minds is by constant reference to them in other kinds of sermons – 'That, after all, is what the Gospel is all about, isn't it?', 'That is what Christ came to do', 'Religion *is* relationship with God. That's what the word means', etc., etc.

PROVIDING A BALANCED DIET

Let us now return to the need for systematic as distinct from what I described as hand-to-mouth, Sunday by Sunday preaching. The pastor's concern in this area is to help his people to know what they believe and why. In days when the majority of people believed in God, belief came easily. The onus of apology lay with the unbeliever. Today the reverse is the situation. It is the Christian who is the odd man out, and he needs to be clear not only about what he believes but why. On what foundations does Christian faith rest? To what convictions about God and man is the Christian committed by the very fact of his being a Christian? And on what foundations do these convictions rest? At what points does the Christian part company most decisively from the non-Christian? The liturgy and its lections presuppose an informed Christian congregation. But there can be few parish priests who are not aware of the gaps and misunderstandings,

the areas of doubt and lack of elementary grasp of basic
Christian affirmations that exist in the minds of many
members of the congregation. This is the situation to which
he must minister, and it dictates the 'pasture' which the
pastor must provide.

'But how', it may be asked, 'can you hope to maintain a
programme of balanced preaching in the circumstances of
today? It might have been possible when you had a full-dress
sermon at Mattins or the mid-morning Eucharist, and
another at Evensong. But the limitations imposed by the
Parish Communion, both of time and the tradition that the
sermon should be related to one or more of the lections, make
any such long-term planning practically impossible.'

I accept the difficulty, but there is one overriding pastoral
consideration to be taken into account, viz. that *for large
numbers of church people the weekly sermon at the Parish
Communion is the only instruction in the Christian faith that
they receive.* We cannot therefore blindly follow a liturgical
tradition, however venerable, without regard to this basic fact
and the responsibility it lays on the preacher. What, then, can
he do? Two things. First, we must adjust our preaching at the
Parish Communion to ensure that it contains a large element
of instruction in the essentials of the Christian faith. We
cannot take for granted this elementary grasp of the Christian
faith, especially where, as in so many parishes today, new and
largely untaught people are adding themselves to the congregation. Secondly, we must provide additional opportunities
for such instruction, which should be both systematic and
also allow for questions and discussion. Let us consider each
of these.

Why should we assume that the Parish Communion offers
less opportunity for a 'full dress' and carefully worked out
sermon than sung Mattins or Evensong? We have already
noted (p. 5) that the sermon in the liturgy does not occupy
the same primacy of place in so far as it is preparatory to, and
is not itself, the climax of the service. But there is no reason to
suppose that it need thereby be diminished in importance.

Word and Sacrament belong together. Each is incomplete without the other. There are two considerations which have combined to reduce the importance of the sermon at the Parish Communion, and both are open to question.

The first is a supposed limitation of time. The presence of children coming with parents and the fact that there is often a large number of communicants have often been assumed to constitute a case for limiting the sermon to five or ten minutes. In the early days of the establishment of the Parish Communion, when a well-attended Evensong offered the opportunity of a longer sermon this appeared a valid argument. But it is now increasingly the custom for separate provision to be made for the children in the vestry or parish hall, at least during the first part of the Eucharist. Also the growing use of lay ministers appreciably reduces the time taken for the administration. There is now little case for the preacher to feel himself prevented from doing full justice to his subject by an imposed and arbitrary time-limit. Moreover, if for the majority of his congregation this sermon is the only instruction they receive in the Christian faith, he and they should be prepared to allow sufficient time to give and to receive it. Exactly what is 'sufficient time' depends on the preacher and his subject, and will doubtless vary from Sunday to Sunday.

While on this point of what may be considered both by the parish priest and his people a due and proper period of time for the Parish Communion, there is one item to which I would like to draw attention and to express a personal view – the intercession. It is my observation that the time allocated to the intercession is often disproportionately long. I have known it to take anything up to ten minutes; far longer than the eucharistic prayer. I offer no comment on the growing practice of handing over this part of the rite (and one or more of the lections) to various members of the congregation, in the desire for increased 'lay participation', except gently to raise an eybrow at this limitation of the notion of 'participation'. What about the rest of the congregation? Are they not equally 'participating'? This is admittedly an aside. The extent to which the incumbent invites his lay folk to share in the celebration of the Eucharist in this way is for him to decide, and it will naturally be bound up with his pastoral policy as a whole. My concern is with the place and time occupied by the intercessions. No one will question that Christians individually and corporately have a duty to pray for the world, and such is the desperate need in every country – Northern Ireland, Africa, Poland, Russia, India, South America, to say nothing of our own divided land, that realistic intercession must involve some attempt to enter imaginatively into the specific situations and needs of each of them. Some place for such extended and detailed intercession should be found in the life of every parish and congregation. But is the Parish Communion the proper setting for it? I suggest that it is not. The gathering of the Lord's people at the Lord's table on the Lord's day is the occasion most demonstrably domestic in the life of the church. Of course we are bidden to pray 'for the Church and the world' because the Church is part of the world. Nevertheless the limitation of time and the need for keeping our thoughts centred upon eucharistic action which has brought us together suggest that we can only do this briefly and in general terms. To fulfil our duty of corporate as well as individual intercession, other opportunity should be provided. It will be said that there is no other time in the week when the whole congregation can come together. There are doubtless many whose duties make it impossible for them to come at any other time. These apart, there are many who could come if they thought it sufficiently important. Most of us are ready to adjust our timetable to fit in with the TV programmes we want to see. If a regular period of corporate intercession is a fixed item in the parish agenda, *some* people will be able to come every time; others may well be ready to share in a rota which commits them to no more than they can manage. Such an arrangement will ensure that at least the whole congregation is represented.

The second and more complex limitation is the tradition

that the subject of the sermon should arise from or at least be related to the liturgical readings appointed for the day, especially now that the compilers of the ASB have linked the readings for each Sunday to particular themes. It is with no lack of appreciation of the care that has gone into the selection of these readings that I strongly maintain that no parish priest should accept them as determining the subject matter of his sermon if the need for the systematic instruction of his congregation requires a course independent of them. Even if the subject matter of the course – on prayer or basic Christian faith, or the place of the Old Testament in Christian spirituality – bears no relation to the proscribed Sunday themes, it seldom requires much ingenuity to make use of or reference to some part of the lections.

With these needs in mind the preacher will be concerned not only with next Sunday's sermon but with the longer term content of his teaching. This involves planning ahead 'This Autumn we must really get down to . . .' The '. . .' to be filled in will be determined partly by pastoral contacts and discovered needs, partly by a review of content of past preaching. This latter makes it essential for the preacher to keep a record of his Sunday by Sunday subject matter. There are various ways of doing this. One is simply to keep a list of his subjects, so that he can quickly look back over the past two or three years to discover what important areas of Christian faith and life he has omitted. I have myself often been astonished to discover how long it is since I preached about some vitally important matter. It takes only a few minutes to write up such a record week by week and it provides the information necessary for planning ahead.

Another way (which may be either an alternative or a useful addition) is to file one's notes or MS under headings of subject matter – God – Christ – the Church – Christian morality – prayer, etc. Some of these files will naturally be much more bulky than others because we find ourselves constantly having to hammer away at fundamental truths. It is nevertheless a quick and convenient way of keeping an eye on the long-term content of our preaching, and as I have already tried to make clear, our policy and purpose in preaching is inseparable from our pastoral policy as a whole.

SUPPLEMENTING THE SUNDAY DINNER

The more aware the pastor is of the pressures under which his people live, and of the secular environment in which they are trying to retain a hold on a distinctively Christian faith and witness, the more obvious it becomes that he cannot hope to discharge his pastoral 'feeding' responsibility solely through the medium of Sunday sermons. That is why the last twenty or thirty years have seen the growth of so many prayer, study and discussion groups meeting on a week night, and which are now regarded as an indispensable part of parish life. They provide an invaluable opportunity for members of the congregation to meet and come to know one another *as fellow Christians,* to share their insights and experiences, to think and pray together about their particular and individual problems. The modus operandi of these groups varies greatly in different parishes, and a consideration of their place and function would take us beyond the scope of this book.

Our immediate concern is with the relation of such groups to the weekly sermon(s) in Church. It is obvious that they are of inestimable value to the parish priest as providing him with the unique opportunity to learn much more than he otherwise might of the real needs of the people he is seeking to serve. Sharing in such groups will both increase his pastoral sensitivity and inform his preaching. Indeed many vicars have experimented in inviting such a group to provide material for, or even to determine the subject of, the Sunday sermon. There is clearly a great deal to be learned from such experiments even if they do no more than help the members of the group to appreciate the responsibility borne by the preacher and the skill he needs effectively to discharge it!

Another and quite common way of relating the group to the sermon is for the group to discuss the implications of the sermon *after* it has been preached. This can be a salutary experience for the preacher. 'Vicar, did you really mean what you said on Sunday, that you can't be a Christian without belonging to the Church, or at least to some Christian body?' Indeed, no matter to what subject the group is addressing itself or what its method of procedure, the chances of some questioning reference to last Sunday's sermon are pretty high, and such an opportunity for a sympathetic 'feedback' is an enormous help and stimulus to the preacher. He will at least learn what pitfalls to avoid!

Where, however, for a period the work of the group is consciously and directly related to the Sunday sermon, I believe that in most cases it is more valuable for the group to do their thinking *before* the sermon rather than after it. This means that the preacher will provide the group with one or more questions germane to the subject of the sermon. The formulation of these questions is clearly important. They must not suggest pious or expected answers but must be designed to provoke the maximum freedom of expression from the members of the group. Let me give you one or two examples of the kind of question I have in mind.

The word 'Gospel' means 'good news'. What of?

In inviting a man to become a Christian, what exactly are we offering *to* him and asking *of* him?

How do you account for the widespread (if veiled) hostility to the Church today? And even among some Christians for the desire for a 'Church-less Christianity'?

What do you think St Paul would have said about the Church in this country?

Do you think that the majority of people today are worried by the fact of death? Or do they avoid facing it?

How widespread is the assumption that death is the end? If people do not think that death is the end, how *do* they think of it?

Those who have wrestled with such questions and probably come to the end of their resources will listen with more than usual attention to what the vicar has to say on Sunday!

Such group experience is of inestimable value both to preacher and congregation. Not only does it provide him with an insight into their real needs, it also gives them the chance to cross-examine him! It also makes it possible for him to answer such questions as lie within his competence *when they arise*. The best time to answer any question is when it is asked.

WEEK-NIGHT COURSES

Nevertheless there is still need for an occasional opportunity to be made for the kind of sustained and concentrated teaching which is possible neither in the Sunday sermon or the week night group. We have already thought of how important it is that our people should have a picture of the Gospel as a whole, and the Bible as a whole, to which they can relate the several aspects revealed by particular sermons and readings. Two ways of trying to meet this need have already been suggested:

1 The occasional sermon giving a summary or birds-eye view of the Gospel or the Bible as a whole – very telescopic indeed but none the less valuable!

2 The short course of three or four consecutive sermons.

There is however a place for something more ambitious than these. I have often been astonished at the number of times when I want to get in touch with a friend or acquaintance engaged in some secular profession, I am told 'I'm sorry, he's not here at the moment. He's away on a course.' Do Christians never need a refresher course? I believe that provision should be made for Christians to go back for what they call in the Navy 'refitting' or overhaul, or refreshment. Not, of course, a residential exercise involving expense and absence from home, but one offered in the parish. How many Christians have had any systematic instruction in Christian faith and life since their preparation for Confirmation – if then?

It may be replied that we do think about fundamental Christian doctrines Sunday by Sunday. But when they are spread over the Christian year there is the risk of losing the thread. By the time we've got to Easter we've forgotten about Christmas, and by Whitsun Good Friday has faded into the past. The result is that we tend to have bits and pieces of Christian truth in our minds rather than a clear picture of the whole.

One way of providing such a refresher course is to set aside a whole week, eight consecutive evenings from Sunday to Sunday, for unashamed basic catechetical instruction. The objection that few people will be prepared to give up a whole week is not borne out by experience. I have myself conducted very many such weeks attended every evening by a large proportion of the Sunday congregation. People will make time for what they regard as important. One week every four or five years is not an excessive demand. I recall one parish in which after such a week the people said, 'This has been so valuable we must make it an annual event'. They did. The second year was given to a course of lectures on the Bible, the third was made a School of Prayer, the fourth (to the best of my recollection) was on the New Testament.

Then there is the opportunity provided by Lent. Mid-week lenten services regarded simply as a devotional extra are losing their appeal. But observation and experience convince me that a weekly mid-week series of straightforward lectures on some important topic will draw a surprisingly encouraging audience. Such a course can be arranged either on a parish or a deanery basis, or mounted in some central church within easy reach of the immediate neighbourhood.

Again, much more use might be made of Sunday evenings. There has been a widespread decline in the number of people who now come regularly to Sunday Evensong. Yet experience has shown that if an occasional opportunity of real help on some specific issue is offered in a course of lectures with opportunity to ask questions (which may or may not be combined with Evensong) during the four Sundays of (say)

March or October many people who do not as a rule come to Evensong will commit themselves to such a limited period. The purpose of all such ventures is concentration on some particular aspect of the Gospel or the Christian life to enable those who share in them to *see as a whole* what can only be treated piecemeal in Sunday sermons.

Even the occasional special 'week-end' is not to be despised. I have known very many such greatly valued by the congregation. It is possible to have several concentrated sessions. The first is on Saturday evening, usually in the parish hall. The second is after a corporate breakfast following the Parish Communion. People then go home to lunch and return to the hall at about 3 or 3.30 for a third session before tea. The fourth session may be in the hall after which people go over to the church either for Evensong or a final session. Local conditions will determine the layout of such a week-end. One of its great advantages is that it provides opportunity for meeting and discussion for a larger number of the congregation than those who can or will take part in a weekly group.

Retreats and retreat addresses fall outside the scope of this book. Suffice to say that in terms of the maximum help that can be received in the shortest available time, there is no doubt that a retreat is by far the best way for Christians to deepen their life in Christ. Since, however, a retreat is concerned primarily with Christian 'spirituality' i.e. with Christian living and praying, it cannot at the same time be occupied with Christian doctrine. The theological foundation must be taken for granted.

It may be objected that the kind of systematic and long-term planned preaching described in this chapter envisages a pastoral situation in which one man is wholly responsible for one congregation or two at the most. This is an ideal which, especially in the rural areas, it is no longer possible to maintain. True. But the experience of many group and team ministries has but served to throw into prominence the need for each congregation to have its own pastor, even if he must be shared with another. Nothing so undermines the confidence of a congregation as not knowing who is going to turn up to take their service, or for pastoral consultation. The greatest complication arises where one priest has to serve two, three or more parishes with the help of readers, and naturally wants to keep personal contact with each of them, which he can only do by constant alternation. In such circumstances it would seem possible to maintain the most elementary scheme of planned preaching only by close co-operation and agreement between incumbent and readers.

How can such corporate planning be reconciled with the principle, earlier stressed in this book, that you can only preach effectively if you *want* to preach on that particular theme? Only, I imagine, if both incumbent and readers are in agreement about the need for some overall planning in their preaching, and each is allowed the freedom to accommodate himself to it as best he can. In whatever pastoral circumstance the preacher may find himself, and however great his awareness of the need for an overall system and long-term planning, the driving force and disposition of every individual sermon should be, 'This is what *I want* to say. May God use it to be received as what *he* wants to say'.

Index